I0411529

United States
Department of
Agriculture

Forest Service

Northern Research
Station

General Technical
Report NRS-P-28

Proceedings
18th U.S. Department of Agriculture
Interagency Research Forum
on Gypsy Moth and Other
Invasive Species, 2007

USDA Interagency Research
Forum on Invasive Species

D'AMICO

January 9-12, 2007 ★ Annapolis, Maryland

ACKNOWLEDGMENTS

Thanks go to Vincent D'Amico for providing the cover artwork.

Proceedings
18th U.S. Department of Agriculture Interagency Research Forum on Gypsy Moth and Other Invasive Species, 2007

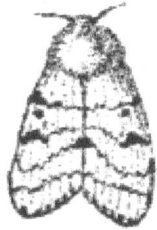
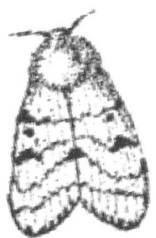

January 9-12, 2007
Loews Annapolis Hotel
Annapolis, Maryland

Edited by
Kurt W. Gottschalk

Sponsored by:

Forest Service Research

Agricultural Research Service

Animal and Plant Health Inspection Service

Cooperative State Research, Education and Extension Service

USDA

CONTENTS

FOREWORD

This meeting was the 18th in a series of annual USDA Interagency Gypsy Moth Research Forums that are sponsored by the USDA Gypsy Moth Research and Development Coordinating Group. The title of this year's forum reflects the inclusion of other invasive species in addition to gypsy moth. The Committee's original goal of fostering communication and an overview of ongoing research has been continued and accomplished in this meeting.

The proceedings document the efforts of many individuals: those who made the meeting possible, those who made presentations, and those who compiled and edited the proceedings. But more than that, the proceedings illustrate the depth and breadth of studies being supported by the agencies and it is satisfying, indeed, that all of this can be accomplished in a cooperative spirit.

USDA Gypsy Moth Research and Development Coordinating Group

Kevin Hackett, Agricultural Research Service (ARS)

Vic Mastro, Animal and Plant Health Inspection Service (APHIS)

Bob Nowierski, Cooperative State Research, Education and Extension Service (CSREES)

Jim Gooder, Forest Service-Research (FS-R), Chairperson

The program committee would like to thank Hercon Environmental, Arborjet, Inc., JJ Mauget Company, and the Management and Staff of the Loews Annapolis Hotel for their support of this meeting.

Program Committee: Mike McManus, Kevin Thorpe, Vic Mastro, Joseph Elkinton, and Therese Poland

Local Arrangements: Katherine McManus

Proceedings Publication: Kurt Gottschalk

CASCADING CONSEQUENCES OF INTRODUCED AND INVASIVE SPECIES ON IMPERILED INVERTEBRATES

David L. Wagner

Ecology and Evolutionary Biology, University of Connecticut, Storrs, CT 06268

The address began with a review of three lists of insects of conservation importance: the U. S. Fish and Wildlife Service's list of 57 federally endangered and threatened insects native to North America (USFWS 2006); Connecticut's Endangered, Threatened and Special Concern Species (CT DEP 2004); and the 26 species of conservation importance identified in Connecticut's recently completed Butterfly Atlas Project (O'Donnell et al. 2007). In addition to the above, information on rare species was extracted from NatureServe (2007), the Red List of Pollinator Insects of North America (Shepherd et al. 2005), and Globally Rare Butterflies and Macro-moths (Lepidoptera) of Forests and Woodlands in the Eastern United States (Schweitzer et al., in prep.).

Non-native invasive species threaten 25 (44%) of the 57 insects listed by USFWS as endangered or threatened, and are second only to development/habitat loss as a threat to listed insects. Invasive species are regarded as the primary threat for 14 of these: 12 Hawaiian *Drosphila*, 1 Hawaiian sphingid moth (*Manduca blackburni* (Butler)), and 1 Californian sphingid moth (*Euproserpinus euterpe* Hy. Edwards). Fire ecology plays an important role in the welfare of many federally listed species, especially among the protected Lepidoptera. Three important threats for vertebrates—overharvesting, pollution, and disease —the third, fourth, and fifth most important factors for imperiled vertebrates (Wilcove et al. 1998), appear to be of minimal importance for insects (but see below).

Principal threats to Connecticut's state-listed insects include a host of factors but two have clear primacy: (1) development + habitat loss and (2) succession + afforestation. Overgrazing by deer was identified as an important but second-order threat. In Connecticut, non-native invasives were regarded to be of tertiary importance, roughly on the same level as excessive ATV and ORV traffic and global warming.

The above approach, focused on state and federally listed taxa, does not take into account that even widespread and common species can become rare and face extinction as a result of biological introductions. A heralded example is that of the apparent displacement of the C-9 lady beetle (*Coccinella novemnotata* Herbst) by the C-7 lady beetle (*Coccinella septempunctata* L.), which in turn appears to have lost ground to the Asian lady beetle (*Harmonia axyridis* (Pallas)) (Stephens and Losey 2003). The recent catastrophic collapse of members of the subgenus Bombus—*Bombus occidentalis* Greene and *B. franklini* (Frisson) in the West and its congener *B. affinis* Cresson in the East, as well as their social parasite, *Psithyrus ashtoni* Cresson—following an epizootic of *Nosema bombi*, that swept through commercial bumblebee hives (Thorp and Shepherd 2005; John Ascher, pers. comm.)[1], was held as a particularly alarming case, illustrating that no species is safe.

The remainder of the talk considered classes of threats to native insects, i.e., those stemming from biological introductions of plants, plant pathogens, inadvertently introduced insects, biological control agents, animal pathogens, and detritovores.

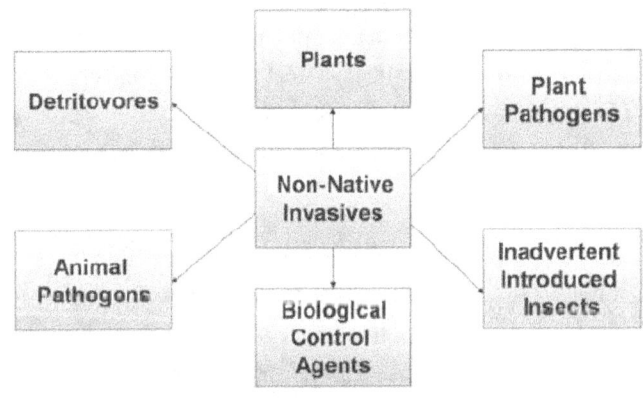

[1] N. American *Bombus* were brought to Europe and reared with European species where transfer of the *Nosema* likely occurred.

The two invasive plants most widely recognized to be threats to state-listed insects in the Northeastern States are common reed (*Phragmites australis*) and purple loosestrife (*Lythrum salicaria*) (Wagner 2007b). Over vast acres New Englanders are witnessing the ecological erasure of diverse wetland communities by these non-natives. A new threat in northeastern woodlands is Japanese stilt grass (*Microstegium vimineum*): from Tennessee to New Jersey, rich forest understories are being replaced by monocultures of stilt grass.

An important invasive plant in non-forested landscapes in the Northeast affecting imperiled insects is autumn olive (*Elaeagnus umbellata*). The shrub is a pernicious invader of early successional habitats, such as sandplains, where many of the region's most imperiled invertebrates are eking out their existence: tiger beetles, ground-nesting bees, sand wasps, ground beetles, and numerous other arenicolous taxa. In part because autumn olive is a nitrogen-fixer, it too often proves to be an early and successful invader of non-vegetated landscapes and accelerates succession.

Partly tongue-in-cheek and partly serious, I introduced the idea of Malcolm effects[2]: Small changes in complex systems that create chain reactions that throw a system from one state into another, the consequences of such are difficult to predict (or control). Citing one example of a Malcolm effect, I talked about instances where exotics have proven to be "egg traps" for rare and declining species: females of the federally endangered sphinx, *Euproserpinus euterpe*, oviposit on filigree (*Erodium cicutarium*) (Family Geraniaceae), a plant on which the larvae have no chance of survival (its normal host is *Camissonia contorta)* (Family Onagraceae)). In the East, garlic mustard (*Alliaria petiolata*) is perceived to be a primary threat to populations of the West Virginia white (*Pieris virginiensis* (W. H. Edwards)) —as garlic mustard invades woodlands, the butterfly disappears.

Introduced plant pathogens are a perennial and chronic threat to our native flora. Five forest diseases that have garnered great attention in eastern North America include beech bark disease, chestnut blight, dogwood anthracnose, Dutch elm disease, and Sudden Oak Death. While all have the potential to change forest stand characters and impact biodiversity, only chestnut blight has been linked to the extinction of insect herbivores. Opler (1978) listed seven American chestnut-feeding lepidopterans as extinct: *Coleophora luecochrysella* Clemens, *Ectoedemia castaneae* Busck, *Ectoedemia phleophaga* Busck, *Synanthedon castaneae* (Busck), *Tischeria perplexa* Braun, *Swammerdamia castaneae* Busck, and *Argyresthia castaneella* Busck. While two of these have since been rediscovered (*Synanthedon castaneae* and *Coleophora leucochrysella*), and the taxonomic validity of two others is in question (*Tischeria perplexa* and *Swammerdamia castaneae*), the remaining three species appear to have been driven to extinction as a consequence of the rangewide collapse of their foodplant, chestnut.

Inadvertently established herbivorous, predatory, and parasitic insects pose great threats to biological communities, especially to those on remote islands and other disharmonic biotas. Hundreds of exotic herbivores have established in the United States—their economic and/ or community-level effects range from largely positive such as honey bee (*Apis mellifera* L.) to potentially devastating such as Mediterranean fruit fly (*Ceratitis capitata*) (Wiedemann) and emerald ash borer (*Agrilus planipennis* Fairmaire). In eastern forests, the gypsy moth (*Lymantria dispar* (L.)) has had no equal in its biological, economic, and even social impacts. Efforts to control this pest are thought to have had direct and indirect consequences for our native lepidopteran fauna.

Other herbivores of great importance to the forests of eastern North America include the hemlock woolly adelgid (*Adelges tsugae* (Annand)) and balsam woolly adelgid (*Adelges piceae* (Ratzeburg)). The destruction of the high-elevation Fraser fir (*Abies fraseri*) forests of the southern Appalachians has been catastrophic. These boreal sky-island communities are home to many endemics, glacial disjuncts (e.g., Scholtens and Wagner 2007), and otherwise globally imperiled species (Keith Langdon, pers. comm.) that are threatened by the changes in forest structure and composition underway as a result of balsam woolly adelgid infestations.

---

[2]Ian Malcolm was the mathematician in Michael Crichton's Jurassic Park who wove fractal and chaos theory into the drama that unfolded on Isla Nublar.

Among three of North America's newest arrivals, the Asian longhorned beetle (*Anoplophora glabripennis* (Motschulsky)), winter moth (*Operophtera brumata* (L.)), and emerald ash borer, the latter is the most worrisome to the conservation community. Early reports suggest the buprestid has the potential to eradicate or greatly reduce ash (*Fraxinus*) from woodlands and forest community types across North America. If the insect's spread and impacts go unchecked, and ash mortality continues to hover near 100%, as many as 21 ash-feeding Lepidopterans could be threatened with extinction (Wagner 2007a). Other indirect effects—cascading consequences—will surely occur. For example, as black ashes are removed from wooded swamps of the Upper Midwest, buckthorn (*Rhamnus cathartica*) is expected to gain a stronger foothold in natural communities.

While much has been written about the impacts of non-native predatory insects on native species, no place has suffered more than Hawaii. Ants, wasps, and insect parasitoids have wreaked havoc on the islands' biota. Forty-seven species of ants have established in Hawaii--included are several of the world's most aggressive pest species. Eighteen percent of the wasps reared by Henneman and Memmott (2001) from native caterpillars retrieved from a high elevation swamp forest represented parasitoid species believed to have been inadvertently established in the Hawaiian Islands.

Purposefully introduced biological control agents have had wide ranging impacts on native species and communities. C.V. Riley's introduction of the Vedalia beetle (*Rodolia cardinalis* (Mulsant)) is held as one of the most successful examples of biological control—the beetle saved California's citrus industry, and impacts to native species appear to have been minimal. In contrast, purposeful introductions of the mongoose to control snakes have proven disastrous for island bird and reptile populations worldwide. Examples of biological control efforts that have impacted indigenous plants and animals have been discussed by Howarth (1991), Van Driesche and Van Driesche (2003), Berenbaum (2004), and others. Several studies have documented consequences of introduced herbivores to our native flora (e.g., Louda and O'Brien 2002). Much recent research has been focused on the non-target impacts of "sanctioned" introductions of

parasitoids. In Henneman and Memmot's (2001) study of the natural enemies of a Hawaiian caterpillar community, introduced biological control agents accounted for 83% of the parasitoids reared from wild, non-target caterpillars. Empirical studies by Benson et al. (2003a,b) provide evidence that the introduced braconid, *Cotesia glomerata* (L.), is at least partially, if not wholly responsible, for the collapse of mustard white (*Pieris napi* (L.)) populations in Massachusetts. Many in New England's conservation community are looking at the tachinid fly (*Compsilura coccinata* Meigan), a generalist and prolific parasitoid of Macrolepidoptera, introduced to control the gypsy moth, as a contributor to the regional decline of silkmoths (Boettner et al. 2000), sphingids, and Datanas.

The ecological impacts of introduced predators, such as lady beetles and vespid wasps, are poorly understood and largely unstudied. Given the millions of Asian lady beetles that turned up in homes throughout the Northeast around the turn of the century, there can be little question that this phenomenally prolific insect had a direct impact on the population dynamics of native predators such as aphelinines, chrysopids, hemerobiids, and even butterflies such as the harvester butterfly, *Feniseca tarquinius* (Fabr.), that were competing for the same food.

Introduced animal pathogens also pose a threat to North American insect biodiversity. A well-documented example was the sudden decline of feral hives of the (introduced) honey bee (*Apis mellifera* L.) across the whole of North America, caused by infestations of the hemolymph-feeding varroa mite (*Varroa jacobsoni* Oudemans). The recent and phenomenally rapid declines of *Bombus franklini* and *B. occidentalis* Greene in western North America and *Bombus affinis* and *B. terricola* Kirby in eastern North America have been linked to a 1998 epizootic of *Nosema bombi* [Microsporidian] introduced through commercial movement of bumblebee queens and colonies for pollination of greenhouse tomatoes (Thorp 2005, Thorp and Shephard 2005).

There is growing concern that even detritovores, and in particular exotic earthworms, dramatically change the terrestrial communities where they establish and proliferate. North America is now home to nearly four dozen exotic earthworm species, some of which (e.g.,

Lumbricus rubellus Hoffm.) are becoming exceedingly abundant and widespread, especially north of the last glacial maximum where native earthworms do not occur. High earthworm densities eliminate surface litter, release elevated amounts of nitrogen, calcify soil, and mix layers that would have otherwise remained largely distinct (Frelich et al. 2006 and references therein). The ecology of the forest understory is fundamentally changed: e.g., studies have documented impacts to understory ferns and herbs (Gundale 2002, Hale 2004, Hale et al. 2006) and amphibians (Migge-Kleiam et al. 2006; John Maerz, pers. comm.).

Some general patterns were then addressed in the talk. Foremost among these was that invasives often loom as focal threats in disharmonic communities, which tend to be ecologically unchallenged and vulnerable to invasion. Remote islands and cave biotas were mentioned as being particularly threatened. Similarly, trophically simplified communities, such as freshwater ecosystems and early successional communities, bear great risk. Conversely, complex and/or ecologically stressful communities —tropical rainforests, tundra, desert, many marine systems—while far from free of non-native invasive species problems, appear to face fewer challenges. Given the above, it is somewhat surprising that our eastern forests ecosystems have so many invasives —perhaps it is just a matter of our forests being challenged by very large species pools, drawing from nearly the whole of Europe and Asia.

In summary, for USWFS-listed species invasives pose the second greatest threat to imperiled insects, second only to development and habitat loss. Invasives are the principal threat facing federally protected species listed from Hawaii. In Connecticut, for both state-listed terrestrial and imperiled butterflies, non-native invasives are of tertiary importance, following afforestation/ succession and deer, and perhaps even global warming in importance. Once exotics are established, expect the unexpected (Malcolm effects): consequences of biological introductions often are complex, indirect, and unpredictable, with problems trickling in and trickling out to other trophic levels. Disharmonic biotas and simple communities are especially threatened by non-native invasives. Exotics pose their greatest threat to biodiversity in those instances where their presence catalyzes changes in basic ecosystem properties—two egregious examples include the impact of the balsam woolly adelgid on the sky island biotas of the southern Appalachians and the changes brought on by introduced earthworms to forest understory communities. If the spread of the emerald ash borer continues unchecked, its ecological consequences will be catastrophic for the many specialist herbivores that rely on ash and the ecological communities where ash is a co-dominant.

Literature Cited

Benson, J.; Pasquale, A.; Van Driesche, R.G.; Elkinton, J. 2003a. **Assessment of risk posed by introduced braconid wasps to *Pieris virginiensis*, a native woodland butterfly in New England.** Biological Control. 23: 89-93.

Benson, J.; Van Driesche, R.G.; Pasquale, A.; Elkinton, J.S. 2003b. **Introduced braconid parasitoids and range reduction of a native butterfly in New England.** Biological Control. 28: 197-213.

Berenbaum, M. 2004. **Friendly fire. Wings.** Essays on Invertebrate Conservation. Spring 2004: 8-12.

Boettner, G.H.; Elkinton, J.S.; Boettner, C.J. 2000. **Effects of a biological control introduction on three nontarget native species of saturniid moths.** Conservation Biology. 14: 1798-1806.

CT DEP 2004. **Connecticut's Endangered, Threatened, and Special Concern Species [Revised Lists].** The Connecticut Endangered Species Act. Chapter 495. General Statutes of Connecticut. Public Act 89-224.

Frelich, L.E.; Hale, C.M.; Scheu, S.; Holdsworth, A.R.; Heneghan, L.; Bohlen, P.J.; Reich, P.B. 2006. **Earthworm invasion into previously earthworm-free temperate and boreal forest.** Biological Invasions. 8: 1235-1245.

Gundale, M.J. 2002. **Influence of exotic earthworms on the soil organic horizon and the rare fern** *Botrychium mormo*. Conservation Biology. 16: 1555-1561.

Hale, C.M. 2004. **Ecological consequences of exotic invaders: interactions involving European earthworms and native plant communities in hardwood forest.** St. Paul, MN: University of Minnesota, Department of Forest Resources. Ph.D. dissertation.

Hale, C.M.; Frelich, L.E.; Reich, P.B. 2006. **Changes in cold-temperate hardwood forest understory plant communities in response to invasion by European earthworms.** Ecology. 87: 1637-1649.

Henneman, M.L.; Memmott, J. 2001. **Infiltration of a Hawaiian community by introduced biological control agents.** Science. 293: 1314.

Howarth, F.G. 1991. **Environmental impacts of classical biological control.** Annual Review of Entomology: 36-485-509.

Louda, S.M.; O'Brien, C.W. 2002. **Unexpected ecological effects of distributing the exotic weevil,** *Larinus planus* **(F.), for the biological control of Canada thistle.** Conservation Biology. 16: 717-727.

Migge-Kleiam, M.; Mclean, A.; Maerz, J.; Heneghan, L. 2006. **The influence of invasive earthworms on indigenous fauna in ecosystems previously uninhabited by earthworms.** Biological Invasions. 8: 1275-1285.

NatureServe. 2007. **NatureServe Explorer: An online encyclopedia of life [Web application]** Arlington, VA. (http://www.natureserve.org/explorer).

O'Donnell, J.E.; Gall, L.F.; Wagner, D.L., eds. 2007. **The Connecticut butterfly atlas.** Hartford, CT: Connecticut Department of Environmental Protection.

Opler, P.A.1978. **Insects of American chestnut: possible importance and conservation concern.** In: McDonald, J., ed. The American chestnut symposium. Morgantown, WV: West Virginia University Press: 83-85.

Scholtens, B.G.; Wagner, D.L. **[In press]. Lepidoptera Great Smoky Mountains National Park: methods of and results of the inventory.** Southeastern Naturalist.

Schweitzer, D.F.; Minno, M.;Wagner, D.L. **[In prep]. Globally rare butterflies and macro-moths (Lepidoptera) of forests and woodlands in the Eastern United States**. USFS Technology Transfer Bulletin, FHTET.

Shepherd, M.D.; Vaughan, D.M.; Black, S.H., eds. 2005. **Red list of pollinator insects of North America.** CD-ROM Version 1 (May 2005). Portland, OR: The Xerces Society for Invertebrate Conservation.

Stephens, E. J.; Losey, J.E. 2003. **The decline of C-9 — New York's state insect**. Wings. Essays on Invertebrate Conservation. Fall 2003: 8-12.

Thorp, R.W. 2005. **Species profile:** *Bombus franklini*. In: Shepard, M.D.; Vaughan, D.M.; Black, S.H., eds. Red list of pollinator insects of North America. CD-ROM Version 1 (May 2005). Portland, OR: The Xerces Society for Invertebrate Conservation.

Thorp, R.W.; Shepherd, M.D. 2005. **Profile: subgenus** *Bombus*. In: Shepherd, M.D.; Vaughan, D.M.; Black, S.H., eds. Red list of pollinator insects of North America. CD-ROM Version 1 (May 2005). Portland, OR : The Xerces Society for Invertebrate Conservation.

USFWS. 2006. **USFWS Threatened and Endangered Species System (TESS)**. http://ecos.fws.gov/tess_public/SpeciesReport.do?kingdom=I&listingType=L&mapstatus=1 (accessed January 2007).

Van Driesche, J.; Van Driesche, R. 2003. **The conundrum of biological control: weighing urgency against uncertainty**. Conservation Magazine. 4(2).

Wagner, D.L. 2007a. **Emerald ash borer threatens ash-feeding Lepidoptera**. Lepidopterists' News. 49: 10-11.

Wagner, D.L. 2007b. **Butterfly conservation**. In: O'Donnell, J.E.; Gall, L.F.; Wagner, D.L., eds. Connecticut butterfly atlas. Hartford, CT: Connecticut Department of Environmental Protection: 287-307.

Wilcove, D.S.; Rothstein, D.; Dubow, J.; Phillips, A.; Losos, E. 1998. **Quantifying threats to imperiled species in the United States.** BioScience. 48: 607-616.

GYPSY MOTH MALES REACTION TO DIFFERENT PHEROMONE CONCENTRATIONS IN SPARSE AND DENSE POPULATIONS

Yuri N. Baranchikov[1], Vladimir M. Pet'ko[1], Amatoliy S. Moiseyev[1], and Victor Mastro[2]

[1]V.N. Sukachev Institute of Forest, Siberian Branch, Russian Academy of Science
50 Akademgorodok, Krasnoyarsk 660039, Russia

[2]USDA Animal and Plant Health Inspection Service,
Otis Methods Development, Otis Air National Guard Base, MA 02542

ABSTRACT

The Asian race of the gypsy moth (GM) (*Lymantria dispar* L.) is the main pest of larch (*Larix*) forests of Mongolia. Variation between habitats in this mountainous country is so high that there is usually no problem in finding insect populations at different stages within a few hours of driving. We worked with two populations of GM. The sparse population was located in the wide valley of the Selenga River covered by *Salix* and *Ulmus* species with larch forests on the slopes of surrounding hills. There were no signs of foliage damage, and we failed to find any larvae and pupae in the tree crowns. An outbreaking GM population was found 200 km southeast of the Selenga River in the Khan-Dzhargalatyn-Uver Valley. The northern slopes of the hills were covered by larch with intensive current-year defoliation. There were a lot of pupae in the tree crowns.

We analyzed responses of GM males to pheromone traps baited with five + disparlure doses of 1, 10, 100, 1,000, and 5,000 micrograms per lure. Cotton swabs with pheromone were prepared in the Otis laboratory and mailed by DHL to Mongolia. The sealed lures were opened and used for only 3 days of experimentation each.

At the beginning of August during GM flight in each habitat, a line of 30 pheromone traps was set (5 traps with each of 5 doses + 5 blank traps). Traps were located in an ABCDEFABCDEF, etc. sequence with 30 to 50 m between traps. We sampled for 3 days in each habitat. We collected moths daily and moved each trap to the next location in the sequence, decreasing influence of relief and stand features on captures.

The reaction of GM males from Mongolian populations on + disparlure was significantly influenced by both population density and pheromone concentration in lures. GM males from the dense population preferred high doses of pheromone (100 and 1000 mcg). In the sparse population, they preferred a lower dose of 10 mcg. Both population density ($F=17.3$; $P=0.0002$) and pheromone dose ($F=3.4$; $P=0.02$) had a significant impact on the captures (two-way ANOVA). The interaction of the factors was also significant ($F=5.0$; $P=0.002$).

The practical outcome of this experiment is promising. This approach may be used to check the gradational status of pest population between outbreaks.

EMERALD ASH BORER HAS REACHED EUROPE

Yuri N. Baranchikov

V.N. Sukachev Institute of Forest, Siberian Branch, Russian Academy of Science
50 Akademgorodok, Krasnoyarsk 660039, Russia

ABSTRACT

Emerald ash borer (*Agrilus planipennis* (Fairmaire) (Coleoptera: Buprestidae)), an introduced aggressive pest of ashes, recently became a nightmare for forest and urban entomologists in the United States. The species originally was known from mixed deciduous forests of Southeastern Asia. The Panel on Quarantine Pests for Forestry of the European and Mediterranean Plant Protection Organization (EPPO) added this buprestid to the EPPO A2 action list as a species of serious risk for the forests of Europe. This prediction came to reality extremely soon after.

In January 2007, recognized Russian taxonomists Drs. A.V. Alekseyev and M.G. Volkovich received a series of specimens of unknown buprestid species of genus Argilus. A few entomologists independently of each other collected live beetles in different regions of Moscow during 2003-2006. Species identity was confirmed by morphological methods. It appeared to be *A. planipennis* previously known only from a few localities in the Russian Far East under its synonym name *A. markopoli* Obenb. The photos of Moscow specimens can be found on the Internet at: http://www.zin.ru/Animalia/Coleoptera/rus/eab_2007.htm. This finding represented the first record of *A. planipennis* in Europe and a major westward range extension for this species.

Fraxinus excelsior and *F. pennsylvanica* are very common on Moscow streets and parks. Trees with 15-20 cm stem diameter and up to 15 m in height predominate. According to the places of collections, the beetle is distributed all over Moscow and its suburbs. Many intensive diebacks of ash trees were recorded in 30 km westwards and southwards from the Moscow Main Ring Road. At some places up to 75% of trees were dead; many of them lost bark and carried D-shaped emerging holes on stems.

There is a huge gap in natural distribution of ash species from the Russian Far East to Eastern Europe. In this territory very few ashes (mainly *F. mandshurica* and *F. pennsylvanica*) can be found in arboretums and private collections. It is believed that

A. planipennis was introduced to the Moscow region at the end of the 1990s with wood packing materials or with growing stock.

Russian quarantine officials are aware of the problem, and an intensive search program will be launched in spring and summer 2007 to estimate the level of pest distribution and injury.

The work on this publication was partially supported by the ALARM Project, funded by the European Commission.

SCREENS FOR RESISTANCE TO *AMYLOSTEREUM AREOLATUM* INFECTION IN LOBLOLLY PINE

John Michael Bordeaux and Jeffrey F.D. Dean

Warnell School of Forestry and Natural Resources
University of Georgia, Athens, GA 30602

ABSTRACT

The wood wasp *Sirex noctilio* and its symbiotic fungus *Amylostereum areolatum* constitute an exotic pathosystem recently introduced into North America (Borchert et al. 2006, Dunkle 2005). Capable of killing living, healthy trees, *S. noctilio* has ravaged pine plantations of the Southern Hemisphere and poses an immediate threat to the conifer forests of the United States, notably the commercially important loblolly pine (*Pinus taeda* L.) (Borchert et al. 2006).

We are working to develop screening methods for identifying resistance to *A. areolatum* fungal challenge in *P. taeda* and other southern pine species. In lieu of testing mature trees, we will use model systems, including pine seedlings, tissue explants, and cultured pine cells. A variety of defense responses to fungal challenge, including accumulation of phenolic compounds, size of lesions, release of active oxygen species, and electrolyte leakage, will be quantified. The goal for this work will be to establish a reliable system for screening *P. taeda* genotypes for innate resistance. Identification of genetic resistance in loblolly or other southern pine species should enable tree improvement programs to mitigate the risk to our commercial pine forests from future *S. noctilio/A. areolatum* outbreaks.

Isolating the effects of *A. areolatum* from those of its insect vector and quantifying their expression represents a meaningful step forward in our knowledge of this pathosystem. Multiple players (wasp, fungus, tree, parasitic nematodes, parasitoids, and possibly others) all contribute to the responses observed in the *Pinus* host. The effects of the combined *S. noctilio/A. areolatum* pathosystem on host trees are well documented. However, the effects of *A. areolatum* alone have not been well characterized on North American pine species. Better understanding of the specific interactions between individual players in this pathosystem will enable us to pursue multiple approaches to subverting key interactions, which should provide a more powerful approach to tree protection. Findings from this study will help establish key steps in the specific interaction of *A. areolatum* with native pines.

Literature Cited

Borchert, D.F.; Fowler, Glenn; Jackson, Lisa. 2006. **Organism pest risk analysis: risk to the Conterminous United States associated with the woodwasp, *Sirex noctilio Fabricius*, and the symbiotic fungus, *Amylostereum areolatum* (Fries: Fries) Boidin**. Raleigh, NC: USDA APHIS-PPQ-CPHST-PERAL: 1-46.

Dunkle, R.L. 2005. **Detection of the European wood wasp, *Sirex noctilio* (*Fabricius*), in New York**. USDA APHIS. p.1.

CURBING INTRODUCTIONS OF FOREST INSECTS AND DISEASES ON NURSERY STOCK

Faith T. Campbell

The Nature Conservancy 4245 North Fairfax Dr., Arlington, VA 22203

ABSTRACT

Since the early 1800s, at least 18 highly damaging forest insects and diseases have been introduced to the United States and its territories via the pathway of trade in living plants.

Half of these pests (those listed on the right side of Table 1) entered the country in the past 35 years. Worse, 6 of those 10 introductions have been detected since 2000: lobate lac scale, Asian cycad scale, *Erythrina* gall wasp, `o`hia rust, cycad blue butterfly, and Pisonia scale.

There is widespread agreement that the current phytosanitary system is not effective in preventing introductions via the live plant trade. (See statements by the USDA Animal and Plant Health Inspection Service, the North American Plant Protection Organization, The International Union of Forest Research Organizations, and The Nature Conservancy.Sources for obtaining these documents are referenced at the end of the paper.)

There is also agreement on the reasons for the rising threat: in recent decades, plant imports have increased greatly, the geographic range of suppliers has expanded, and more rapid transport allows more pests to survive transit. At the same time, phytosanitary safeguards have been relaxed rather than tightened.

Table 1. Forest pests introduced via the trade in living plants since 1800

- *Phytophthora cinnamomi*	Dogwood anthracnose - *Discula destructive*
Chestnut blight - *Cryphonectria arasitica*	Sudden Oak Death - *Phytophthora ramorum*
White pine blister rust - *Cronartium ribicola*	Bromeliad weevll - *Metamasius callizona*
Balsam woolly adelgid - *Adelges piceae*	Citrus longhorned beetle - *Anoplophora chinensis*
Port-Orford-cedar root disease - *Phytophthora lateralis*	Lobate lac scale - *Paratachardina lobata lobata*
Beech scale - *Cryptococcus fagisuga*	Pisonia scale - *Pulvinaria urbicola*
European Viburnum leaf beetle - *Pyrrhalta viburni*	Asian cycad scale - *Aulacaspsis yasumatsui*
Hemlock woolly adelgid - *Adelges tsugae*	*Erythrina* gall wasp - *Quadrastichus erythrinae*
Butternut canker - *Sirococcus clavigignenti - juglandacearum*	`o`hia rust - *Puccinia psidii*
	Cycad blue butterfly - *Chilades pandava*

The U.S. phytosanitary system currently relies largely on inspection. When USDA APHIS becomes aware of a sufficient risk, it conducts a pest risk assessment of one or a few genera from a particular country.

Both approaches have significant weaknesses. Regarding inspection, APHIS, NAPPO, and IUFRO agree that current trade volumes overwhelm inspection capacity. The NAPPO Concept Paper notes that inspectors experience great difficulty in detecting pathogens, small pests, pests at low densities, pests living inside the plant, or if symptoms are masked by pesticides.

Pest risk analysis has several problems. First, it is resource intensive. APHIS has admitted that the agency has insufficient funds to complete risk assessments and amend regulations in a timely response to newly perceived threats.

Second, and more troubling, risk assessments are severely limited in identifying threats. As the NAPPO and IUFRO papers have pointed out, risk assessments based on lists of known quarantine pests do not address uncertainties arising from
• Organisms not known to science
• An organism's behavior in its native environment is a poor predictor of its behavior when introduced to a new environment
• Increased risk when the pest or pathogen hybridizes

An effective exclusion program must prevent introductions of pests that are unknown or insufficiently understood, and it must be implemented **quickly** to curb the current, unacceptable rate of introductions.

The NAPPO and IUFRO papers both noted the importance of preventing introductions of organisms that have not been thoroughly studied. The history of introductions supports the concern: at least six of the most damaging forest pathogens that entered the country on imported plants were unknown to science when they were introduced. These were *Cryphonectria parasitica*, *Phytophthora lateralis*, *Discula destructive*, *Phytophthora cinnamomi*, *Phytophthora ramorum*, and *Sirococcus clavigignenti-juglandacearum*.

International trade rules adopted under the auspices of the World Trade Organization (WTO) and the International Plant Protection Convention (IPPC) require that phytosanitary regulations be applied **only** to pests that have been evaluated by pest risk assessments. The only exception is provisional regulations. These risk assessments must evaluate risks with great specificity. Even "pathway" risk assessments must evaluate each pest using the pathway as to its specific likelihood of entry, establishment, or spread. These rules appear to impede effective exclusion policies by tying regulatory action to the time-consuming and scientifically limited risk assessment process.

There is widespread agreement on the structure of a long-term solution to the challenge of preventing introductions of organisms that are too poorly known to be evaluated in a risk assessment. That solution is to institutionalize clean stock or best management practices programs that will minimize the presence not just of quarantine pests (those identified through risk assessment) but also most insects, pathogens, and other potential pests that have not been evaluated. The IUFRO panel suggests that adoption by

Table 2. USDA APHIS chart showing changes in plant import conditions since the "Q-37" regulations were first adoptedd

Trading Partners	Europe	Worldwide
# of Items Allowed Import	Limited (< 100 items) germplasm of clonal material only	Unlimited
Fumigation	Mandatory on all imported stock	Only when quarantine pest found
Likely Purpose of Importation	Nursery propagation program "starter" material **Slow distribution**	Direct field/homeowner planting **Immediate distribution**

the IPPC parties of an international standard (modeled after the international standard on wood packaging) would allow clean stock programs to apply to the full range of pests, not just quarantine pests. As its rationale, the IUFRO panel notes that the living plant pathway has been the means by which many pests have been introduced—just as wood packaging has been. This parallel situation justifies a similar response: reliance on a pathway approach that departs from the usual blacklist approach.

This proposal has great promise—particularly because an IPPC expert group is already exploring whether to recommend an international standard for living plant movement. However, it is not certain that the IPPC parties will accept such a broad standard.

In any case, negotiating and implementing effective clean stock programs will require several years. We need stringent measures to curtail introductions **now** to protect our forests until IPPC parties can negotiate and implement a comprehensive program.

USDA APHIS has proposed the solution: placing plants suspected of carrying pests **temporarily** into a limbo category pending further evaluation and development of effective phytosanitary barriers. APHIS could do this quickly. Because plants are placed in limbo on an interim or "provisional" basis, APHIS would not be required to complete a pest risk analysis on each plant/origin combination before acting.

Unfortunately, APHIS intends to phase in the limbo category. Initially, only the few plant host/origin combinations that transport known quarantine pests would be included and even then only when the plants in question have not previously been imported into the U.S. Only after several years might APHIS expand the category to address pests whose existence is unknown or whose ecological role in their native and introduced ranges has not been adequately assessed.

The Nature Conservancy believes that APHIS should apply its conception of a limbo category more
· aggressively, given the recent rush of introductions. The Conservancy proposes that APHIS take the following steps:

(1) Publicly adopt a goal of providing a much higher level of protection. APHIS should state its intention of cutting the rate of introduction via this pathway to one-tenth of its apparent current level—from 10 species over 30 years to only 1.

(2) By the end of 2007, establish a strong NAPPRA category and put into that category nearly all whole plants and cuttings. APHIS could allow imports of these plant taxa under any of the following conditions:

• plants imported in the form of tissue culture or seed
• plants imported into a secure containment facility and held for a sufficiently long period to ensure they are pest- and disease-free
• plants imported from a third-party certified clean stock program.

(3) Apply a transparent process to determine which taxa/type/origin combinations are sufficiently unlikely to transport pests that they can be removed safely from NAPPRA.

(4) Focus its risk assessments on the most likely introductory pathways, which would be defined, such as bare-rooted plants from East Asia.

(5) APHIS and its stakeholders should work together to secure substantially more staff and funding to enable the agency to undertake risk analyses and amendments to its regulations in a timely manner.

Sources of further information:

APHIS Whitepaper (December 2005) http://www.aphis.usda.gov/import_export/plants/plant_imports/downloads/q37_whitepaper.pdf

(If the link doesn't work, try using your favorite search engine to search for "Addressing the Risks Associated with the Importation of Plants for Planting")

NAPPO Plants for Planting Concept Paper--attached to RSPM 24 at http:/www.nappo.org/Standards/NEW/RSPMNo24-e.pdf

IUFRO Working Party on Alien Pest Movement in International Trade

Accessible on www.forestresearch.gov.uk/iufroinvasives

The Nature Conservancy. An Ounce of Prevention: How to Stop Invasive Insects and Diseases from Destroying U.S. Forests, fcampbell@tnc.org

CONSIDERATIONS IN ROBOTIC INVASIVE CONTROL: TREE-OF-HEAVEN[1]

Robert Daley

Department of Computer Science, University of Pittsburgh,
5401 Sennott Square, Pittsburgh, PA 15260

ABSTRACT

This paper describes the motivation, premises, and research plan for the Foresbott Project (http//www.cs.pitt.edu/~daley/foresbott/). The goal of the Foresbott Project is the development of autonomous robots that can navigate forests and carry out tasks associated with maintenance of forest health, including detection and control of invasive species, in particular, tree-of-heaven (*Ailanthis altissima*). Briefly, the physical capabilities (hardware) of robots are much farther advanced than the behavioral capabilities (software). The approach to the development of robotic behaviors suitable for forest health tasks is described along with results from earlier work by the author on the co-evolution of robot behaviors for tasks in a different application (Daley and Grefenstette 1996).

Motivation

The importance of forests cannot be overstated. Yet, the number of assaults on our forests by invasive species is increasing dramatically. In Pennsylvania most of the forest land is privately owned, but the majority of landowners don't address the issue of forest health. Moreover, parcelization of forest land and logging activities often promote the spread of invasives. But robotics offers a solution. Imagine a robot that could navigate a forest, identify a problem (e.g., a tree-of-heaven), and take corrective action (e.g., apply herbicide). Imagine further that it was possible (e.g., through some governmental grants program) for forest landowners to deploy this robot to periodically maintain the health of their forest. This is the goal of the Foresbott Project. There are many other applications for such a robot were it to be developed, including military surveillance, and search and rescue.

Premises

A great deal of progress has been made in the field of robotics. The physical capabilities (hardware) of robots have advanced dramatically. One example of this is the Big Dog robot developed by Boston Dynamics (http://www.bostondynamics.com/). However, the ability to develop complex behaviors (software) for robots is far less advanced. For example, the DARPA program "Learning Locomotion" (BAA05-25) has the goal of developing control software that will enable a robot (viz., Boston Dynamics Little Dog) to move across rough terrain. The approach is to develop algorithms that will enable the robot to "learn" this software (It is expected that the performance of the algorithms developed will far exceed the performance of handcrafted systems, creating a breakthrough in locomotion over extreme terrain). The Foresbott Project will also develop its robotic behaviors using learning algorithms.

Research Plan

The development of a robot that can navigate forests, identify invasive species, and take corrective action is indeed a very ambitious undertaking, one that will take decades to complete. The strategy that has been adopted here is to develop those aspects that are specific to forestry applications (navigating in a forest, identifying invasive species, taking corrective action) and to complement that effort with state-of-the-art improvements in other aspects of robotics and artificial intelligence. Rather than undertake the costly effort of building and testing a robot in a forest, we will initially work with simulated robots in a simulated forest environment.

[1]This work supported in part by U.S. Forest Service Project FHP-FHTET-TD.01.M01.

Robot Morphology

Most creatures that navigate forests have legs, sometimes many of them, so it seems reasonable that the forest robot will be legged. But, how many legs? This will have to be determined as part of the platform development. Likewise, numerous other physical aspects (morphology) of the robot must be determined for the forest robot. Included in these are number and types of joints, size of the robot, lengths of inter-joint segments, sensors, and actuators. Each of the three major functional components of the robot (navigation, identification, and corrective action) requires its own set of sensors and actuators. Navigation sensors will include an (active) vision system, sonar, infrared, LIDAR, touch sensors, electronic whiskers, and possibly others. Most of these types of sensors have been studied widely.

Sensors for identifying invasive species are specific to the forest health application and will include a (passive) vision system, an electronic nose (of some type) and a spectrophotometer or spectroradiometer, and possibly others. For example, the tree-of-heaven has a distinctive smell that might be detected by an electronic nose. Multispectral analysis has had some success in identifying tree species from airplanes, but it remains to be determined whether these techniques can be used for identifying tree-of-heaven at ground level. Identification using computer vision is an obvious choice, but in general object recognition using computer vision is very difficult. Considerable experimental effort needs to be made to ascertain which combination of sensors will enable the robot to detect invasive species. Finally, the robot will need sensors and actuators (as yet to be determined) that will allow it to take corrective action, e.g., apply herbicide to a tree-of-heaven specimen.

Robot Behaviors

Each of the three major functional components will also need complex control software. This we view as an assemblage of interconnected robot behaviors. As in the DARPA Learning Locomotion Project, we plan to "learn" this assemblage of behaviors. We will be using co-evolutionary algorithms to learn most of the (lower-level) robotic behaviors. To be sure, other techniques from artificial intelligence (e.g., planning) will have to be used also. The particular learning system to be used is the SAMUEL genetic algorithm (GA) system developed by John Grefenstette (Grefenstette 1990) at the Naval Center for Applied Research in Artificial Intelligence (NCARAI) of the Naval Research Laboratory. In fact, we will be using the SAMUEL system to co-evolve both the behaviors and the morphology of the robot. We briefly mention some previous work (Daley et al. 1999, 2007) dealing with the co-evolution of robot behaviors using the SAMUEL system.

In Daley et al. 1999, 2007 we built a two-dimensional simulator for the Nomadic (wheeled) Robot and used SAMUEL to co-evolve a complex task consisting of two somewhat conflicting goals of tracking a second robot and periodically docking at a recharging station. We considered several regimes for co-evolving this complex behavior. One, the Monolith regime, consisted of one GA that tried to learn the entire behavior. Our results showed that this complex task could not be learned as a whole (Fig. 1). We also studied several regimes where the task was decomposed into three behaviors: a tracking behavior, a docking behavior, and an executive behavior that decided periodically which task to perform. Our results showed that for most of these decomposition regimes the complex behavior was successfully learned (Fig. 2). Our main purpose in these studies was to determine the best regime for the co-evolution of this complex task. The relevant aspect of this work for the Foresbott Project is that complex behaviors, if properly decomposed, can be learned using co-evolutionary methods.

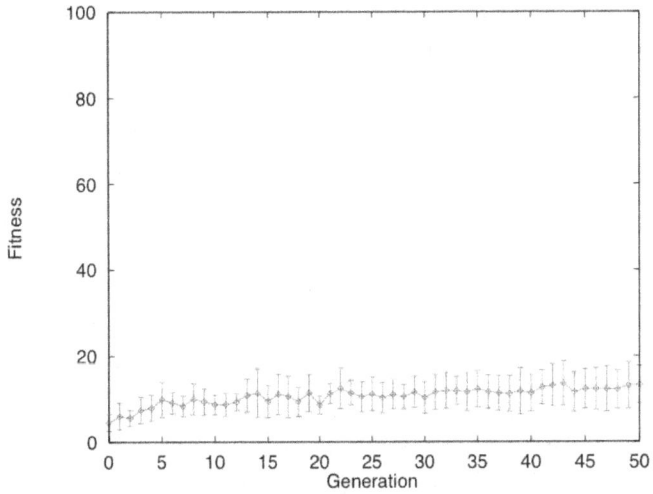

Figure 1. Monolith Learning

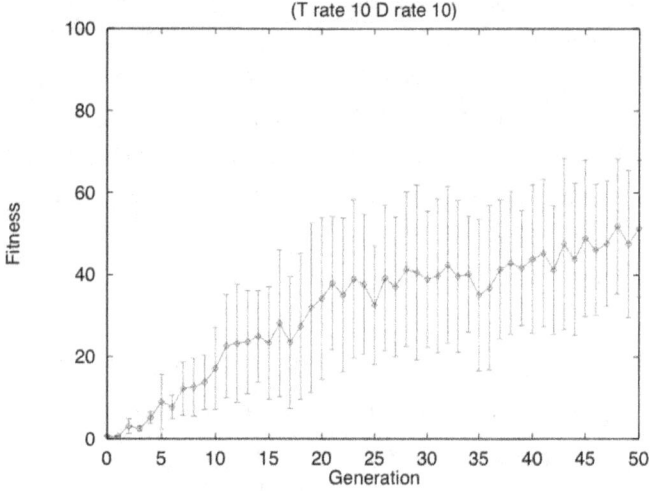
(T rate 10 D rate 10)

Figure 2. Decomposed Learning.

Over the last few years the author has been developing at NCARAI a distributed computation platform for the SAMUEL system that will run on cluster computers and that will allow co-evolutionary methods to be applied to large-scale problems, i.e., complex tasks consisting of a large number of interconnected behaviors. The requirements for this platform involve fault-tolerant computing within a network of computers, because there will be many GAs simultaneously and jointly evaluating their populations over an extended period of time. This is critical for the co-evolution of our forest robot behaviors.

Simulation Tools

The initial phases of the Foresbott Project will work with simulated environments. There are many advantages to this approach. First of all, it is much less costly to simulate a robot than to build one and test it (and possibly damage it, and have to repair it). Second, because we plan on learning the robot behaviors, using a real robot would take too long – learning on a simulated robot, where time can be sped up, is the preferred approach. Similarly, we plan to evolve the robot's morphology as well, and "tinkering" with small changes in the robot's physical components would consume an inordinate amount of time. Finally, a robot simulator can "fake" unsolved problems. For example, developing robotic vision is an extremely hard problem and for a real robot could prevent progress on many of the other behaviors. In a simulated environment, development of the vision component can be postponed until further

progress on the robotic vision problem is made. Instead, the simulation's god's eye view can be used to pass information to the behaviors that depend on the vision system.

The real challenge in using a simulated robot is in finding high-quality simulators for the robot and its sensors and actuators. For legged robots, a three-dimensional simulator that can perform the necessary kinematics (physics) calculations is essential. Fortunately, such simulators are available and we describe two such here. The first is the Open Dynamics Engine (ODE) (http://www.ode.org). ODE provides the basics for three-dimensional simulations including several types of joints and the corresponding kinematics. In addition, several simulation systems use ODE as their basis but provide simulation software for many of the sensors that are of interest including pan-tilt-zoom (ptz) cameras, sonar, and LIDAR. Included in this list are Player-Stage http://sourceforge net/projects/playerstage),URBI (http://www.urbiforge.com/), and Webots (http://www.cyberbotics.com/).

However, other possible sources of 3D simulators are computer game engines. Of particular promise is the Unreal Tournament Game (UT2004) (http://www.epicgames.com/). The Urban Search And Rescue Simulation (USARSim) (Lewis et al. 2007) (http://sourceforge net/projects/usarsim), currently being maintained by NIST, is built on top of the UT2004 platform. One important consideration for this approach is that the next version of Unreal Tournament (UT2007) will use the AGEIA physics coprocessor(http://www.ageia.com/). This will considerably speed up the simulations and allow for more complex environments. However, because we will be using the simulator for learning robot behaviors, it is important that the simulation clock can be run at a rate that is faster than real time. Finally, the Microsoft Corporation (http://msdn microsoft.com/robotics/) has begun development of a robotics development platform that will also use the AGEIA physics coprocessor. One interesting feature of Microsoft's approach is that its simulations will use software emulation (via the AGEIA PhysX SDK) in case the coprocessor is not installed.

In conclusion, the Foresbott Project is a very ambitious undertaking, but one that in the long run will be worthwhile.

Literature Cited

Daley, R.; Grefenstette, J. 1996. **Methods for competitive and cooperative co-evolution.** Adaptation, co-evolution and learning in multiagent systems workshop; 1996 AAAI Symposium; 1996 March 25-27; Stanford University.

Daley, R.; Grefenstette, J.; Schultz, A.1999. **Co-evolution of robot behaviors**. SPIE International symposium on intelligent systems and advanced manufacturing (ISAM '99); 1999 September 19-22; Boston, MA.

Daley, R.; Grefenstette, J.; Schultz, A. 2007. **Methods for co-evolution in multi-behavior robots.** Unpublished manuscript.

Grefenstette, J.J.; Ramsey, C.L.; Schultz, A.C. 1990. **Learning sequential decision rules using simulation models and competition.** Machine Learning. 5 (4): 355-381.

Lewis, M.; Wang, J.; Hughes, S. 2007. **USARSim: simulation for the study of human-robot interaction.** Journal of Cognitive Engineering and Decision Making, Santa Monica, CA : HFES. 1 (1): 98-120.

AN INDEPTH LOOK AT NEW VIRAL STRAINS FOR USE IN GYPCHEK

Vincent D'Amico[1], James Slavicek[2], John Podgwaite[3], Kevin Thorpe[4], Ralph Webb[4],
Roger Fuester[5], and Randy Peiffer[6]

[1]U.S. Forest Service, Northern Research Station, Department of Entomology and Wildlife Ecology
University of Delaware, Newark, DE 19717

[2]U.S. Forest Service, Northern Research Station, 359 Main Rd., Delaware, OH 43015

[3]U.S. Forest Service, Northern Research Station, 51 Mill Pond Rd., Hamden, CT 06514

[4]USDA Agricultural Research Service, Beltsville Ag. Research Center, Beltsville, MD 20705

[5]USDA Agricultural Research Service, Beneficial Insect Rearing Lab, 501 S. Chapel St., Newark, DE 19713

[6]Delaware State University, AGNR, Dover, DE 19901

ABSTRACT

Gypchek is a baculovirus-based insecticide produced by the U.S. Forest Service. This biopesticide is species-specific to the gypsy moth (*Lymantria dispar*) and contains as an active ingredient the *Lymantria dispar* nucleopolyhedrovirus, also known as the gypsy moth virus or LdMNPV. Currently, Gypchek is a mixture of many strains of LdMNPV, produced in vivo and refined into a usable product at our facility in Ansonia, CT. From 2003 to 2006, we conducted a number of field experiments designed to determine if a single strain of LdMNPV might be a suitable replacement for the current mixture. Additionally, research has been conducted in Delaware, OH (J. Slavicek[2]) toward producing the virus in vitro.

Central to our testing methodology was the bugs-in-bags experiment. In these experiments, virus was applied to branches as infected first-instar larvae OR as a sprayed product. Branches with approximately 40 leaves were selected on oak trees in the Cedar Swamp State Wildlife Management Area near Smyrna, DE. These branches were then enclosed in mesh bags with 25 third-instar test larvae, representing bugs that would be eating contaminated foliage in the field. After 1 week in the field, branches were cut off trees, returned to the lab, and test larvae were removed to individual diet cups. They were reared in the cups for 3 weeks and necropsied if they died. See below for numbers of larvae used in each experiment.

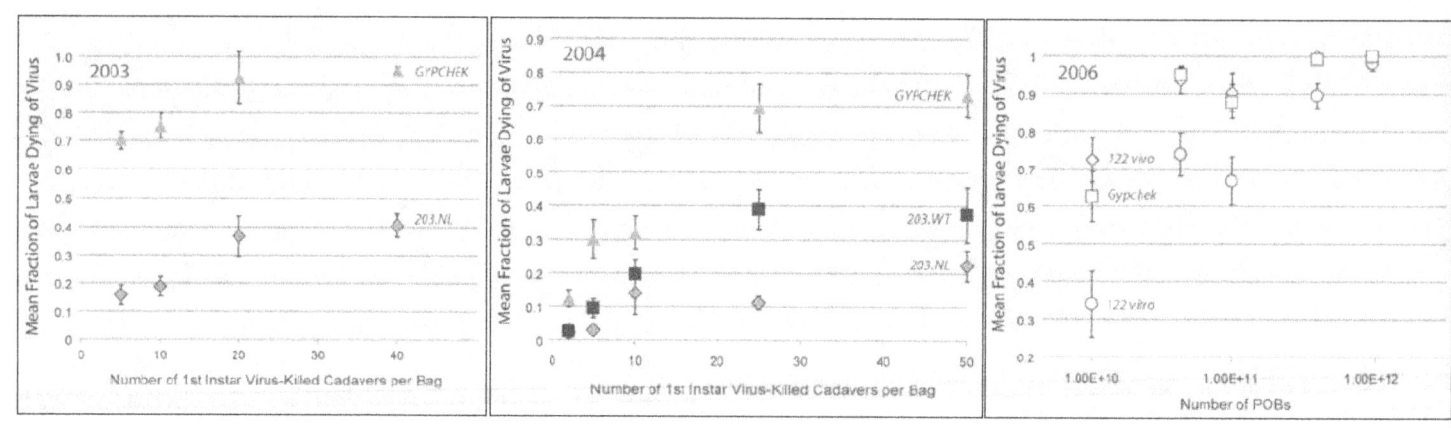

LIVING WITH EMERALD ASH BORER: WHICH TREES WERE ATTACKED FIRST IN MICHIGAN'S UPPER PENINSULA?

Tara L. Eberhart and Andrew J Storer

Ecosystem Science Center, School of Forest Resources and Environmental Science
Michigan Technological University, 1400 Townsend Dr., Houghton, MI 49931

ABSTRACT

The exotic emerald ash borer (EAB) (*Agrilus planipennis)* (Coleoptera: Buprestidae) is established in Lower Michigan and some surrounding states. At high population densities, all green, black, and white ash trees are apparently susceptible to attack and can be expected to die. The first record of this insect in Upper Michigan was from Brimley State Park in the eastern Upper Peninsula of Michigan. In the fall of 2005, as part of an ongoing risk-based detection survey, larvae were extracted from a trap tree that had been used at the site since 2004. The insect was most likely introduced via infested firewood. Subsequently, an eradication effort was made by cutting and removing all of the ash trees within one-half mile of the infested trees. This provided the opportunity to identify additional infested trees within the park and to collect disks from all trees for growth ring analysis.

Disks were cut from a total of 53 white ash (*Fraxinus americana*) trees, selected from within the park, including 7 in which EAB larvae were found. An additional five trees in the park were also found to contain EAB larvae, but did not have disks cut from them and therefore only tree diameter information is available for those trees. Dendrochronology was used to determine whether tree age, tree size (diameter), or tree growth affected the likelihood of EAB larvae being present in an ash tree in the early stages of infestation when the population density is still relatively low. By testing the ranks of ash trees and using non-linear regression techniques, we found that age and tree size were significantly related to the presence of EAB larvae, with the larger, older trees more likely to be infested. Radial tree growth (mean basal area increment) was also lower on attacked trees.

These findings have potentially important implications for design of detection surveys for EAB, because adult landing rates may be higher on larger older trees, and larvae are apparently more likely to be found in larger older trees during the early stages of an infestation. This information, along with other information on the efficiency of trap trees, needs to be considered in future detection efforts.

LIVING WITH EMERALD ASH BORER: ASH REDUCTION MODELS AS SILVICULTURAL TOOLS

Tara L. Eberhart, Andrew J. Storer, and Linda M. Nagel

Ecosystem Science Center, School of Forest Resources and Environmental Science
Michigan Technological University, 1400 Townsend Dr., Houghton, MI 49931

ABSTRACT

The exotic emerald ash borer (*Agrilus planipennis*) (Coleoptera: Buprestidae) is established in a number of states, including Michigan, Indiana, and Ohio, and in one Canadian province, Ontario. At high population densities, all green, black, and white ash trees are apparently susceptible to attack and can be expected to die. Emerald ash borer larvae develop in the phloem of ash trees in stems and branches above approximately 2.5 cm in diameter. Removal of ash from high priority areas such as those stands in close proximity to outlier populations will reduce the population density of this insect.

The surface area of over 500 ash trees was measured using standing trees as well as cut trees throughout Lower and Upper Michigan. White, green, and black ash trees in open-grown and forested settings were all represented. There are strong quadratic relationships between diameter at breast height and calculated surface area of the tree, but these quadratic relationships differ significantly between open-grown and forest-grown trees when the different ash species are considered. Multiple models have been developed for use in management prescriptions to reduce the amount of ash available to emerald ash borer. These models are based on ash species and crown light exposure. Information on ash species and the light exposure for most of the trees in a stand (i.e., forested or open-grown trees) may allow managers to use a more specific model to fit their stand.

Other relationships between diameter, surface area, and volume of phloem are being determined. These relationships, in addition to others involving tree vigor, form, and growing conditions, have been integrated into models characterizing the amount of ash phloem in a forest stand. Using these models with density information (trees per acre) from a stand and stock table, we can determine diameter limits for cutting to meet prescribed ash phloem reduction targets. By reducing emerald ash borer populations through phloem reduction, and decreasing the removal of the smaller trees in a stand, this model will enable the genetic diversity of ash to be optimized during ash reduction efforts. Similar models are available for use when the management goal is to retain large trees within a stand. Applied models help land managers to make scientifically quantifiable decisions relating to ash reduction in forests. Forest resource managers are able to access the models online at www.ashmodel.org and determine the diameter limit for removal of ash to achieve the phloem reduction target within the context of other forest management goals.

EVALUATING LURES TO DETECT SIRICIDS INFESTING CONIFERS OF THE SIERRA NEVADA AND THE ALLEGHENY MOUNTAINS: POTENTIAL FOR TRAPPING *SIREX NOCTILIO*

Nadir Erbilgin[1], John Stein[2], Robert Acciavatti[2], Carline Rudolph[3], Nancy Gillette[4], and David L. Wood[1]

[1]Division of Organisms and Environment, University of California, Berkeley, CA

[2]U.S. Forest Service, Forest Health Technology Enterprise Team, Morgantown, WV

[3]U.S. Forest Service, Forest Genetics Lab, Placerville, CA

[4]U.S. Forest Service, Pacific Southwest Research Station, Berkeley, CA

ABSTRACT

The European wood wasp (*Sirex noctilio*) has become established in several countries in the Southern Hemisphere where North American pine species are widely used in plantations. Therefore, S. noctilio may pose a threat to North America's conifer forests, e.g., especially Monterey, loblolly, slash, lodgepole, and ponderosa pines. Wood wasps of the genus Sirex and other genera are well represented in the forests of North America. Our objective was to characterize variation in the behavioral chemistry of wood wasps in the Central Sierra Nevadas in California and the Alleghenies in West Virginia.

We tested several compounds during 2004-2006 using various release devices that were attached to flight intercept traps. Chemicals and release devices were provided by ChemTica Internacional (Son Jose, Costa Rica). We tested monoterpenes [(-)-α-pinene, (+)-α-pinene, (-)-β-pinene, and (+)-3-carene] in September-October 2004 and different classes of terpenoids [monoterpene hydrocarbons ((-)-alpha-pinene, (-)-beta-pinene, 3-carene), alcohols ((-)-cis-verbenol, (+)-cis-verbenol and (-)-trans-verbenol, (+)-trans-verbenol), aldehydes ((-)-myrtenol, (+)-myrtenol, geranial), ketones (pinocarvone, fenchone, verbenone)] in July-October 2005. Based on the results obtained in 2005, we tested fenchone, (+)-3-carene, (+)-3-carene + fenchone, (+)-3-carene + ethanol, (-)-α-pinene + ethanol, sirex lure (a mixture of α-pinene and β-pinene), ethanol, and a blank control in June-October 2006.

The most abundant species caught were *Sirex areolatus*, *S. behrensii*, *S. cyaneus*, *S. longicanda*, *Urecerus californicus*, and two unknown species in California, and *S. cyaneus*, *S. edwardsii*, *S. nigricornis*, *U. cressoni*, and *Tremex columba* in West Virginia. Our 3-year study indicated that (-)-α-pinene in combination with ethanol or 3-carene alone attracted significantly more wood wasps than the control and the remaining treatments. Although ethanol is not attractive to wood wasps, it synergized attraction to (-)-α-pinene. These results suggest that (-)-α-pinene plus ethanol and (+)-3-carene alone are the most promising attractants for native wood wasps. We plan to conduct a release rate study of these compounds in 2007 and to test these compounds in forests where *S. noctilio* is present.

BIOLOGICAL IMPACT OF AND CONTROL MEASURES FOR COGONGRASS IN THE SOUTHEASTERN UNITED STATES

Wilson H. Faircloth[1], Michael G. Patterson[2], and James H. Miller[3]

[1]USDA Agricultural Research Service, National Peanut Research Laboratory, P.O. Box 509, Dawson, GA 39842

[2]Department of Agronomy and Soils, Auburn University, Auburn, AL 36849

[3]U.S. Forest Service, Southern Research Station, 520 Devall Dr., Auburn, AL 36849

ABSTRACT

Cogongrass (*Imperata cylindrica* (L.) Beauv.) is a non-native, invasive weed that is disrupting economically and ecologically important plant communities in the southeastern United States. Cogongrass accidentally entered the U.S. at several locations, one of which was near Grand Bay, AL, in Mobile County, around 1911. Since that time, this aggressive, perennial, warm-season grass has infested over 200,000 ha in southern Alabama, Mississippi, and Florida. Several intentional introductions have been documented, and unauthorized acquisitions from these areas also account for many hectares of infestation in central and southern Florida and in certain areas of Mississippi. Cogongrass, known also as speargrass, japgrass, or alang-alang, causes damage in forests, rights-of-way, protected natural areas, industrial lands, tree and fruit crops, and soil disturbance following its establishment is usually minimal. Due to the intensive tillage commonly practiced in row crop agriculture, cogongrass has yet to become a serious pest in this industry. Cogongrass is particularly damaging to forested land because it decreases biodiversity and wildlife habitat, hinders plantation establishment, creates a wildfire hazard, and is assumed to decrease wood and fiber production. Effective control and management treatments are critically needed by forest landowners and managers for rehabilitating cogongrass-infested lands. Tree plantations have been established in Asia to aid rehabilitation and could hold promise for reclaiming infested lands in the Southeast. The primary research objective of this project was to investigate integrated vegetation management options for the establishment and/or reforestation of loblolly pine (*Pinus taeda* L.) into cogongrass-infested areas.

The study site was located in Mobile County, AL. The experiment was a factorial arrangement that tested two herbicide site preparation (SP) treatments, two mechanical SP treatments, and two pine release herbicide treatments. Herbicide SP levels were none and a broadcast-applied tank mixture of glyphosate at 3.3 kg ae/ha, imazapyr at 0.34 kg ae/ha, and nonionic surfactant at 0.5 % v/v. Application was on October 3-4, 2001. Mechanical SP levels were a scalping treatment and none. Scalping consisted of using a bulldozer and fire plow to remove the upper 10 to 15 cm of cogongrass rhizomes and roots, folding these back upon intervening grass to create a furrow in which seedlings were planted. Scalping was performed on December 19, 2001. Release treatment levels were band-applied herbicide and none and were applied after seedling planting. In addition to the eight plots in the factorial core, a ninth treatment, termed "complete control," was added. The nine treatments were replicated four times in a randomized complete block design. Bare-root, improved loblolly pine seedlings were hand-planted on January 15, 2002.

Biomass Response

In the year immediately following planting of trees, mechanical SP reduced biomass in each category. However, in the following year, regrowth occurred to an extent that mechanical SP made no treatment differences. The combination treatment of mechanical and herbicide SP reduced live grass by 98.5% compared to the non-treated check in the first year, which suggests greater than an additive effect when combined compared to a single use. Live cogongrass regrew by eightfold to eighteenfold by the second year on all SP treatments, and all treatments contained live grass at the 2003 harvest (780-7400 kg/ha). Other woody and herbaceous plant biomass was least in the non-treated (830 kg/ha) and greatest in the complete control (8310 kg/ha). Herbicide SP and complete control yielded the greatest recruitment of other woody and herbaceous species in both years to assist with the rehabilitation process (8310 kg/ha in year two). The herbicide SP yield was significantly greater than both the mechanical SP and the non-treated, while mechanical SP yielded woody and herbaceous biomass equivalent to the non-treated. Data analysis revealed few significant differences between treatments or establishment methods for live grass and other species at year two. Despite intensive control efforts, cogongrass remained a significant component of the plant community as live cogongrass made up at least 15% of the total plant biomass through year two. Herbicide SP resulted in at least 30% other species, increasing the overall plant community diversity in those treatments.

Tree Response

Loblolly pine survival was equal to or exceeded 90% on all treatments including the non-treated check in years one and two after planting. Treatments with herbicide SP had greater survival, either with or without mechanical SP or release. Site preparation, whether herbicide or mechanical, yielded a significant increase in ground-line diameter (GLD) compared with no SP, while the addition of release made no difference in GLD in the first year. On average, herbicide SP and release showed an additive effect for GLD response. Tree height in year one ranged from 46.1 to 66 cm. Herbicide SP yielded 6-cm taller trees than mechanical SP unless combined with mechanical SP, in which case an antagonistic effect

was found. The negative interaction of mechanical SP and herbicide SP was significant for both loblolly pine GLD and HT. One possible explanation for this response is that soil, previously treated with SP herbicides, sloughed into the mechanically created furrows, thus concentrating herbicide around the seedlings. Stunting of the trees resulted along with a visual yellowing of needles during the first growing season. This effect was evident in both treatments that received herbicide SP followed by mechanical SP. Effects were transient, however, and not observed during the second growing season. Site preparation significantly increased tree growth in the second year by all measures compared to no SP. Aside from the non-treated trees, the release only treatment consistently yielded the smallest trees. For HT only, herbicide SP yielded taller trees than did mechanical SP. These data suggest that 2 years after application, herbicide SP is positively influencing loblolly pine growth more than the other establishment techniques. Release alone was not as effective as other establishment techniques because trees were generally smaller than those treated with SP.

Summary

Herbicide SP consistently increased loblolly pine growth, decreased live cogongrass, and increased overall plant community diversity. Release alone was not an effective reforestation technique; however, it was generally additive when combined with an SP treatment. The use of herbicides was critical to the recruitment of woody and herbaceous species other than cogongrass. No reforestation technique reduced cogongrass to acceptable levels; however, the establishment of loblolly pine was successful, so some productivity was restored to the land.

SUDDEN OAK DEATH AND *PHYTOPHTHORA RAMORUM:* AN UPDATE ON RESEARCH WITH IMPLICATIONS FOR REGULATIONS AND MANAGEMENT

Susan J. Frankel

U.S. Forest Service, Pacific Southwest Research Station, 800 Buchanan St.
West Annex Building, Albany, CA 94710-0011

ABSTRACT

In 2006, Sudden Oak Death mortality, caused by the exotic, invasive plant pathogen *Phytophthora ramorum* (Werres, Cock, & Man in't Veld), surged along the central California coast from Monterey County north to Humboldt County. The recent increase in tanoak (*Lithocarpus densiflorus* [Hook. & Arn.] Rehder) and coast live oak (*Quercus agrifolia* [Nee]) mortality has been driven by two consecutive wet springs, which greatly increased spore loads (Rizzo, pers. comm), followed by exceptionally hot summers. This pattern of mortality has just recently been understood and is explained by the pathogen's ability to ramify through the xylem, thereby disrupting water relations (Brown and Brasier 2007, Parke et al. 2006b). It is becoming clear that the mode of action for *P. ramorum* is that of a wilt disease. Trees are not killed by girdling cankers, but rather by an impaired ability to meet their water needs.

After 5 years of research, funded primarily via the U.S. Forest Service Sudden Oak Death/*P. ramorum* extramural, competitive, research program, scientists are making significant new discoveries. Some research highlights and their management implications are listed below. For more information on these investigations, and on Sudden Oak Death, go to the California Oak Mortality Task Force Web site at www.suddenoakdeath.org.

Finding: The natural infection of tanoak seedling roots by *P. ramorum* was first detected (Parke et al. 2006a).

Implications: *P. ramorum* may enter plants by moving from the soil through roots. *P. ramorum* movement may not be limited to aboveground, aerial dispersal. *P. ramorum* may be present in fine roots of tanoak, as well as boles.

Finding: Camellia buds harbor *P. ramorum* (Tjosvold et al. 2006).

Implications: Camellia buds need to be inspected for symptoms. On camellia, *P. ramorum* infections may persist in the buds rather than leaves, as was previously thought, because infected leaves abscise fairly quickly once infected. Buds may play a greater role in pathogen survival and spread than previously realized.

Finding: *P. siskiyouensis* (Reeser and EM Hansen), a new *Phytophthora* species, has been recovered from soil and water in southwest Oregon (Reeser et al. 2006).

Implications: Many new *Phytophthora* species are being discovered. Will they cause widespread disease in a forest somewhere in the world? Was this species present and previously undetected, or is it new?

Finding: Multiple molecular analyses have identified distinct lineages of *P. ramorum* throughout its known range in forests and nurseries and demonstrate that it was introduced to both the United States and Europe (Ivors et al. 2006.

Implications: *P. ramorum* is moving in nursery stock. It is not native to the United States or Europe. Three distinct evolutionary lineages have been introduced to U.S. nurseries. One of the three lineages has become established in California and Oregon forests, and another lineage has become established in several European forests. The third lineage has not yet been found in a forest.

Finding: The *P. ramorum* genome was annotated revealing an exceptionally large repertoire of secreted proteins

(Tyler et al. 2006). *P. ramorum's* genome was sequenced less than 4 years after the organism was discovered, the shortest time for any species. *P. ramorum* has 15,743 genes, while *P. sojae* ([Kaufm. & Gerd.], soybean *Phytophthora*) has 19,027 genes.

Implications: *P. ramorum,* like other *Phytophthoras*, has a diverse array of proteins with which to attack plants. *Phytophthora* species are Stramenopiles and belong to a kingdom distinct from plants, fungi, and animals. They are closely related to diatoms, brown algae, and Saprolegnia, a salmon parasite.

Literature Cited

Brown, A.V.: Brasier, C.M. 2007. **Colonization of tree xylem by *Phytophthora ramorum, P. kernoviae* and other *Phytophthora* species**. Plant Pathology. 56: 227–241.

Ivors, K.; Garbelotto, M.; Vries, I.D.E.; Ruyter-Spira, C.; Heckkert, B.TE.; Rosenzweig, N.; Bonants, P. 2006. **Microsatellite markers identify three lineages of *Phytophthora ramorum* in US nurseries, yet single lineages in US forest and European nursery populations**. Molecular Ecology. 15: 1493–1505.

Parke, J.L.; Bienapfl, J.; Oh, E.; Rizzo, D.; Hansen, E.; Buckles, G.; Lee, C.; Valachovic, Y. 2006a. **Natural infection of tanoak seedling roots by *Phytophthora ramorum.*** Phytopathology. 96: S90.

Parke, J.L.; Oh, E.;Voelker, S.; Ochiai, N.; Hansen, E. 2006b. ***Phytophthora ramorum* reduces xylem sapflow and specific conductivity of sapwood in mature tanoak.** Phytopathology. 96: S90.

Reeser, P.W.; Sutton, W.C.; Hansen, E.M. 2006. ***Phytophthora siskiyouensis,* a new species from soil and water in southwest Oregon.** Phytopathology. 96: S97.

Tjosvold, S.A.; Chambers, D.L.; Thomas, S.L.; Blomquist, C.L. 2006. **First report of *Phytophthora ramorum* infecting *Camellia* flower buds in North America.** Online at: http://www.plantmangementnetwork.org/php/elements/sum.asp?id=5447 & photo = 3089. Plant Health Progress DOI:10.1094/PHP-2006-0825-01-BR.

Tyler, B.M.; Tripathy, S.; et. al. 2006. **Genome sequences uncover evolutionary origins and mechanisms of pathogenesis.** Science. 313 (5791): 1261-1266.

EVALUATION OF PUBLIC AWARENESS OF ISSUES RELATING TO FIREWOOD MOVEMENT AND THE EXOTIC EMERALD ASH BORER IN MICHIGAN

Janet L. Frederick and Andrew J. Storer

Ecosystem Science Center, School of Forest Resources and Environmental Science Michigan Technological University, 1400 Townsend Dr., Houghton, MI 49931

ABSTRACT

The exotic emerald ash borer (*Agrilus planipennis*) was first identified in Michigan in 2002 and has killed millions of ash trees (*Fraxinus* spp.) there and in surrounding states. A key goal in management of emerald ash borer is to reduce the insect's artificial spread to new locations through its movement in firewood. The movement of firewood is now regulated in some infested states, as well as in some uninfested ones. Inspections of firewood in state and federally operated campgrounds have revealed that ash firewood is still being used and is likely being moved around Michigan. Public education campaigns have been implemented to inform people about emerald ash borer and the associated firewood regulations. These educational programs use fliers, billboards, radio and television advertisements, newspaper articles, and television documentaries, and other media.

During the summer of 2006, two types of questionnaire-based surveys were conducted at state park campgrounds throughout Michigan to (1) determine public awareness of the regulations associated with the movement of firewood, (2) determine any demographics that influence a patron's knowledge about the firewood regulations, and (3) identify the components of the educational program that are reaching the most campground patrons. The first type of questionnaire was distributed at selected state parks and self-administered by campground patrons. The second type of questionnaire was administered by a researcher at selected state parks.

Based on the results of the researcher-administered questionnaires, approximately one-quarter of campground patrons bring their own firewood with them, and of these about one-quarter travel over 200 miles to camp. Most campground patrons (95%) are aware that there are regulations relating to the movement of firewood, and when asked if they had heard of emerald ash borer, almost 91% indicated that they had. The researcher-administered surveys also revealed that patrons are hearing about emerald ash borer and the firewood regulations through educational outreach programs. The results of these questionnaire-based surveys will help focus future efforts on the outreach methods that are apparently the most effective in educating the public about emerald ash borer.

BIOLOGY AND HOST SPECIFICITY OF *GONIOCTENA TREDECIMMACULATA* (COLEOPTERA: CHRYSOMELIDAE): A POTENTIAL BIOLOGICAL CONTROL AGENT FOR KUDZU

Matthew J. Frye, Judith A. Hough-Goldstein, and Clifford B. Keil

Department of Entomology and Wildlife Ecology, University of Delaware, Newark, DE 19717

ABSTRACT

Gonioctena tredecimmaculata (Jacoby) (Coleoptera: Chrysomelidae) was sent from China to the United States for testing as a potential biological control agent of kudzu (*Pueraria montana* var. *lobata* (Willd.) Maesen & S. Almeida). In quarantine, adult females kept on kudzu produced 2-6 larvae per day by ovoviviparous reproduction. Insect development was rapid, with larval and pupal stages lasting 5.6 ± 0.08 and 9.6 ± 0.13 days at 25 °C, respectively. Larvae consumed a total of 16.3 ± 0.63 cm^2 of kudzu foliage per day, while adult beetles consumed approximately 5 cm^2. Newly emerged adults fed on foliage for approximately 15 days before burrowing in the soil for an apparent obligate diapause. These beetles mated and reproduced the following year.

Preliminary host-range tests examined insect feeding on a limited number of native and agriculturally important plants related to kudzu under no-choice conditions. Both adults and larvae of *G. tredecimmaculata* rejected most of the plants that were tested, but fed on soybean (*Glycine max* (L.) Merr.) and American hog-peanut (*Amphicarpaea bracteata* (L.) Fernald) in addition to kudzu. In a supplemental study, insects showed similar responses to field-grown and greenhouse-grown soybean and kudzu foliage despite measurable differences in leaf traits. Field foliage of both plants exhibited greater leaf toughness, higher total carbon content, higher trichome density per mm^2, and reduced water content compared to greenhouse foliage. Further tests are needed in China to determine if feeding on non-target host plants will occur under more realistic, open-field conditions.

INSECTS CONTRIBUTING TO ASH MORTALITY
IN EASTERN PENNSYLVANIA

R. W. Fuester[1], P. B. Taylor[1], and J. A. Wildonger[2]

[1]USDA Agricultural Research Service, Beneficial Insects Introduction Research
501 South Chapel Street, Newark, DE 19713

[2]Department of Entomology and Wildlife Ecology, University of Delaware
Townsend Hall, Newark, DE 19711

ABSTRACT

Because of reports of extensive ash mortality in eastern Pennsylvania, we began surveys for emerald ash borer (EAB) (*Agrilus planipennis* Fairmaire) at Tyler State Park in Bucks County. We sampled trees scheduled for takedown at two locations in the park having old mature and younger trees, respectively. Trees marked for takedown were clearly in poor condition, having numerous beetle exit holes and signs of woodpecker attacks. Virtually all the beetle exit holes were round, typical of cerambycids, and only a few D-shaped exit holes were seen, but these were smaller than the 3-4 mm holes left by EAB adults. At the request of the park manager, we removed bark only from trees marked for takedown. Beetle feeding galleries were very extensive on mature trees, far more so than on the younger trees. Most of the galleries were tightly packed with frass, with little evidence of sawdust at the base of trees.

Clearly the most frequently encountered beetle was the ash and privet borer (*Tylonotus bimaculatus* Haldeman). Because the adults are active only during May-August, we recovered only a few dead adults of this species. However, we recovered quite a few larvae that ranged in age from nearly neonate to full grown, which is consistent with the beetle's 2-year life cycle. Young larvae of *T. bimaculatus* feed in the phloem, but later tunnel deeper, scarring the wood. In addition, they pack frass behind them as they feed, leaving no external signs of their activity. This species attacks both living and dying trees, and usually kills large branches before attacking the trunk. Old, mature, and drought-ridden trees growing in parks and windbreaks (such as those we observed at Tyler State Park) can be killed by this species. Larvae of *T. bimaculatus* readily accepted our artificial diet. No other cerambycids were recovered in these initial surveys. Additional sampling should result in the recovery of banded ash borer and redheaded ash borer.

No larvae of EAB or other buprestids were recovered in these initial surveys. Although we anticipate that EAB is more likely to be recovered in western Pennsylvania because of its proximity to the generally infested area in the Great Lakes region, it would be unwise to declare Tyler State Park EAB-free based on these meager results. Therefore, we intend to assist the Pennsylvania Forest Pest Management in additional survey efforts.

THE DYNAMICS OF EASTERN HARDWOOD FORESTS WITH AND WITHOUT BEECH BARK DISEASE

Jeffrey Garnas[1], Matthew Ayres[1], and Celia Evans[2]

[1]Biological Sciences, Dartmouth College, 103 Gilman Hall, Hanover, NH 03755

[2]Adirondack Watershed Institute, Paul Smith's College, Paul Smiths, NY 12970

ABSTRACT

The spread of beech bark disease (BBD) through eastern North America has had a strong impact on the structure and function of the forest ecosystem, beginning some time after the introduction of the beech scale, *Cryptococcus fagisuga* Lind. (Homoptera:Eriococcidae), in 1890. Stands infected by beech scale and by one or more associated species of the ascomycete genus *Neonectria* typically exhibit adult tree mortality approaching 50% within the first 10 years post-infection (Houston 2005). Despite early predictions that beech (*Fagus grandifolia* Ehrh.) would be removed from the forest canopy, the species has maintained a strong presence throughout most of its range and has even increased in basal area in some stands (Leak 2006). A long-standing hypothesis that BBD enhances the production, growth rate, and/or survival of root sprouts provides a plausible mechanism for the persistence of the species (Held 1983, Houston 1975). We used Forest Inventory and Analysis (FIA) data to examine how the spread of BBD may interact with tree reproductive strategy to alter the size and age structure of forest stands. We analyzed stand trajectory over time with respect to expectations from the self-thinning curve (Fig. 1) and tested how the direction of change with respect to the mean size and density of trees differed in the presence versus absence of BBD, relative to the proportion of beech in the stand.

We parameterized thinning curves for each state and for all states combined using $\log_{10}$-transformed estimates

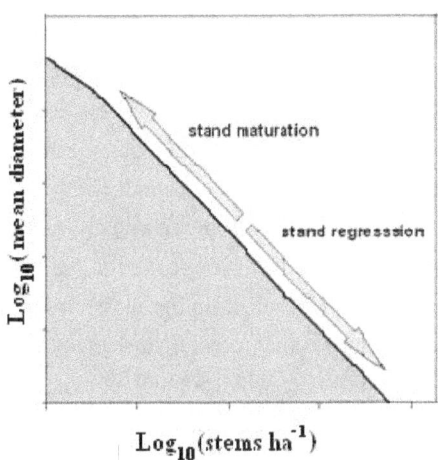

Figure 1. Theoretical representation of a self-thinning curve, showing alternate stand trajectories over time.

of mean diameter and stem density at the first measured cycle, limiting our dataset to all plots containing >1% beech basal area that were sampled two or more times in the past 25 years. We used the regression line estimate for the 95th quantile as the thinning curve boundary (slope = -0.33 ± 0.04; Cade and Guo 2000, Cade and Noon 2003, Koenker 2005). Boundary slopes did not differ among 20 of 22 states and approximated the theoretical expectation of -4/9 (corrected from -4/3 to reflect a linear measure on the Y-axis), widely cited in studies of self-thinning in plants (White and Harper 1970, Yoda et al. 1963). Normal stand maturation corresponds to movement either toward the thinning curve boundary (tree growth/increased mean diameter) or along the boundary in the direction of fewer, larger stems (tree growth plus self-thinning, or a decrease in stem density due to competition for light or nutrients in a closed canopy). "Stand regression" was defined as movement along the same boundary line in the opposite direction, corresponding to a reduction in mean tree size and/or an increase in the number of stems over time. We calculated stand trajectory as the Euclidean distance between matched plots at $time_1$ and $time_2$ relative to the thinning curve boundary, assigning a positive value to stand maturation and a negative value to stand regression. To our knowledge, this is the first analysis of forest dynamics in eastern North America that takes advantage of the spatially extensive and scientifically selected study sites in FIA data. A surprising general result was that stands closest to the thinning curve boundary at $time_1$ were significantly more likely to move in the direction of stand regression. Because this is opposite the predicted pattern of tree growth and self-thinning in the absence of disturbance, it implies that forest disturbance of various kinds may be more widespread than expected. Mechanisms that could be contributing to this pattern include pests and pathogens, harvesting of mature and overmature stands, and changes in biogeochemistry (e.g., nitrogen deposition and calcium depletion) that tend to produce mortality of large trees in relatively mature stands.

Results were consistent with the a priori prediction that a greater proportion of stands in BBD-infected forests moved in the direction of stand regression. That is, within regions with a relatively long history of BBD, but not in regions that have lacked BBD, there was a significant increase in the variance in stand trajectory as % beech basal increase. The statistical support was that the slopes of forest maturation by BBD basal area increased from the 10th to the 90th quantiles (Koenker 2005) where BBD was present (BBD-present: $F = 10.7$, $df = 1,1719$, $P = 0.001$) but not where BBD was absent ($F = 0.9$, $df = 1,3235$, $P = 0.33$). In the spring of 2007, I will seek to conduct additional tests by including another FIA cycle in the analyses, and by explicitly considering effect of latitude and year of scale insect establishment on variation in stand trajectory. These data provide strong initial support for the role of BBD in dramatically altering the size and age structure of stands throughout its range.

Literature Cited

Cade, B.S.; Guo, Q.F. 2000. **Estimating effects of constraints on plant performance with regression quantiles**. Oikos. 91: 245-254.

Cade, B.S.; Noon, B.R. 2003. **A gentle introduction to quantile regression for ecologists.** Frontiers in Ecology and the Environment. 1: 412-420.

Held, M.E. 1983. **Pattern of beech regeneration in the East-Central United States**. Bulletin of the Torrey Botanical Club. 110: 55-62.

Houston, D.R. 1975. **Beech bark disease aftermath forests are structured for a new outbreak**. Journal of Forestry. 73: 660-663.

Houston, D.R. 2005. **Beech bark disease: 1934 to 2004...Or, what's new since Ehrlich?** In: Beech bark disease: Proceedings of the beech bark disease symposium; 2004 June 16-18; Saranac Lake, NY. Gen. Tech. Rep. NE-331. Newtown Square, PA: U.S. Department of Agriculture, Forest Service, Northeastern Research Station: 138-141.

Koenker, R. 2005. **Quantile regression.** Cambridge, New York: Cambridge University Press.

Leak, W. 2006. **Fifty-year impacts of the beech bark disease in the Bartlett Experimental Forest, New Hampshire**. Northern Journal of Applied Forestry. 23: 141-143.

White, J.; Harper, J.L. 1970. **Correlated changes in plant size and number in plant populations**. Journal of Ecology. 58: 467-&.

Yoda, K.; Kira, T.; Ogawa, H.; Hozumi, K. 1963. **Self-thinning in overcrowded pure stands under cultivated and natural conditions**. Journal of Biology of Osaka City University. 14: 107-129.

WHEY-BASED FUNGAL MICRO-FACTORIES FOR IN SITU PRODUCTION OF ENTOMOPATHOGENIC FUNGI

Stacie Grassano and Scott Costa

Department of Plant and Soil Science, University of Vermont, Burlington, VT 05405-0082

ABSTRACT

Whey-based fungal micro-factory technology is being developed to overcome economic and physical constraints associated with use of mycopathogens for management of insects and other pests. This novel formulation technology is based on inclusion of whey as a nutritive substrate to allow bio-control fungi to grow and multiply post-application. Laboratory experiments using the entomopathogen *Lecanicillium muscarium* applied to either sterile Petri dishes or field-collected hemlock foliage produced dramatic increases in number of entomopathogen spores (Fig. 1). Extensive fungal growth was noted on treated hemlock foliage, which upon re-isolation was identified as *L. muscarium*. This species of fungus has activity against hemlock woolly adelgid *(Adelges tsugae)*, an invasive pest causing serious damage to the eastern hemlock and Carolina hemlock. Mycotal, an EU-registered product containing *L. muscarium*, is being researched for U.S. registration and deployment for management of hemlock woolly adelgid.

The dramatic increases in spore concentration in treatments that contain whey demonstrate the potential for whey-based fungal micro-factories to increase post-application abundance of bio-control fungi, such as *L. muscarium*. The observation that micro-factory production can be inhibited in treatments with high spore concentrations indicates that formulations must be optimized for maximal in situ production. This technology may be applicable to fungal bio-control agents other than entomopathogens (insect-killing fungi), such as mycoherbicides and fungi for management of mites, diseases, and nematodes attacking plants.

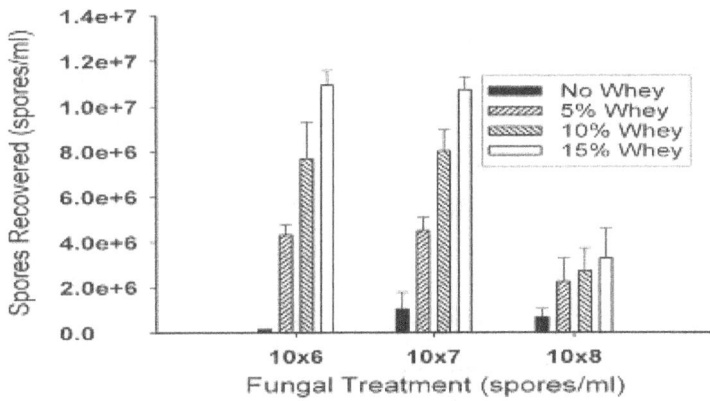

Figure 1. Spores recovered from Petri dish lids after 7 days of micro-factory production at the initial spore and whey concentrations indicated. The "no whey" treatments are the controls.

HOW RISKY IS BARK THAT IS ASSOCIATED WITH TREATED WOOD PACKING MATERIAL?

Robert A. Haack and Toby R. Petrice

U.S. Forest Service, Northern Research Station, 1407 S. Harrison Rd., East Lansing, MI 48823

ABSTRACT

Many of the bark- and wood-infesting insects that have become established outside their native ranges were likely transported in wood packing material (WPM) such as pallets, crating, and dunnage (Haack 2006). WPM, especially in past decades, was often made from untreated, low-grade green lumber that had much residual bark. In recognition of this phytosanitary threat, the international community adopted standards for treating WPM in 2002 that are referred to as "International Standards for Phytosanitary Measures No. 15" or simply ISPM-15 (FAO 2002). Originally there were two approved treatments—heat treatment (minimum core temperature of 56°C for 30 min) and fumigation with methyl bromide—but others such as microwaves may follow (FAO 2002, Keiran and Allen 2004). These treatments are aimed at killing insects and disease organisms that reside in the wood at the time of treatment. Currently, ISPM-15 allows bark to be present on treated WPM; however, it is not known if insects can infest WPM after treatment, especially when bark is present.

We conducted studies in 2004 and 2005 to investigate whether insects would infest recently milled green logs and lumber that had varying amounts of bark. This study was conducted as part of an international collaborative effort under the auspices of the "International Forestry Quarantine Research Group" (http://www forestry-quarantine.org). In 2006, we conducted surveys of foreign WPM marked with the ISPM-15 logo that arrived at six U.S. ports-of-entry to estimate the percentage of the WPM that contained bark and live insects of quarantine significance. Other details of these projects were published recently as extended abstracts (Haack et al. 2007a,b)

In the 2004 log study that tested three hardwood species and one conifer, Cerambycidae and Scolytidae infested and reproduced in fully barked logs after heat treatment, often at densities higher than in the non-treated control logs. In the 2005 study that used only red pine boards, Cerambycidae and Scolytidae laid eggs in all sizes of bark patches that were tested (about 25, 100, 250 and 1,000 cm^2) after heat treatment, but did not infest control or treated boards that had no bark. Cerambycidae completed development in only those boards with bark patches of about 1000 cm^2, while Scolytidae completed development in bark patches of 100, 250, and 1000 cm^2.

In the 2006 survey in which nearly 6,000 individual pallets, crates, and pieces of dunnage were evaluated at six U.S. ports, approximately 9.4% of the wood items contained some bark, and of those with bark about 1.2% contained live insects under the bark, for an estimated overall infestation rate of all WPM of 0.1% (0.1% = 9.4% x 1.2%).

These studies indicate that insects of quarantine significance can infest and develop in bark patches on WPM after heat treatment, although the actual infestation rate of WPM marked with the ISPM-15 logo is relatively low.

Literature Cited

FAO (Food and Agriculture Organization). 2002. **International standards for phytosanitary measures: guidelines for regulating wood packaging material in international trade**. Pub. 15. Rome, Italy: Food and Agriculture Organization of the United Nations.

Haack, R.A. 2006. **Exotic bark- and wood-boring Coleoptera in the United States: recent establishments and interceptions.** Canadian Journal of Forestry Research. 36: 269-288.

Haack, R.A.; Petrice, T.R.; Nzokou, P. 2007a. **Do bark beetles and wood borers infest lumber following heat treatment? The role of bark**. In: Gottschalk, K,W., ed. Proceedings, 17th U.S. Department of Agriculture interagency research forum on gypsy moth and other invasive species; 2006 January 10-13; Annapolis, MD. Gen. Tech. Rep. NRS-P-10. Newtown Square, PA: U.S. Department of Agriculture, Forest Service, Northern Research Station: 46.

Haack, R.A.; Petrice, T.R.; Nzokou, P.; Kamdem, D.P. 2007b. **Do insects infest wood packing material with bark following heat-treatment?** In: Evans, H.F.; Oszako, T., eds. Alien invasive species and international trade. Warsaw, Poland: Forest Research Institute: 145-149.

Keiran M.; Allen, E. 2004. **Keeping forest pests from moving around the world.** Unasylva. 217: 29-30.

DISPERSAL OF GYPSY MOTH PATHOGENS INTO AREAS NEWLY COLONIZED BY GYPSY MOTH

Ann E. Hajek[1], Joshua Hannam[1], Charlotte Nielsen[1], Andrea Diss-Torrance[2], Ken Raffa[3], and Patrick Tobin[4]

[1]Department of Entomology, Cornell University, Ithaca, NY 14853-2601

[2]Wisconsin Department of Natural Resources, P.O. Box 7921, Madison, WI 53707

[3]Department of Entomology, University of Wisconsin, Madison, WI 53706

[4]U.S. Forest Service, Northern Research Station, 180 Canfield St., Morgantown, WV 26505

ABSTRACT

As gypsy moth colonizes new areas, the fungal and viral pathogens infecting larvae also disperse into new gypsy moth populations. Our study addresses spatial and temporal conditions associated with pathogen dispersal to answer questions about predictability of pathogen dispersal. Larval pathogens were investigated along the edge of gypsy moth spread in central to southwestern Wisconsin in 2005 and 2006. Each year, in six intensive sample sites, we collected larvae and cadavers from the field, we caged larvae at these sites and, in the laboratory, we exposed larvae to field-collected soil. During the field season, we added appropriate sites but only some of these procedures were used at the added sites.

The most sensitive sampling method for detecting pathogens was collecting larvae in the field and rearing them, but this method required dense enough populations so that larvae could be found. In 2005, the majority of intensive sample sites were in areas with <30 male moths per pheromone trap the previous year; few gypsy moth larvae were found and, among caged larvae, very little infection occurred. In 2005, *Entomophaga maimaiga* infections were found in three of nine total sites, with NPV present at two sites. In 2006, intensive sample sites were located in areas with 3 to >100 males moths per pheromone trap; more larvae could be collected and more infection by both pathogens was found. *E. maimaiga* infections were found in 6 of 12 sites, with NPV at 5 of the sites. For both years, *E. maimaiga* infections were usually more abundant than NPV infections when the pathogens co-occurred. There was a clear association between distance from the nearest quarantined county and presence and percent infection of pathogens. No infections were found in 2005 sites with very low density gypsy moth populations (< 1 male moth/trap). The only sites outside of quarantined counties where we found pathogens were locations with >10 male moths/trap the previous year where larvae could easily be collected. Within quarantined counties, where gypsy moth populations were generally more abundant, pathogens were usually, but not always, found. In one instance demonstrating the variability within quarantined counties where gypsy moth populations are present but frequently not abundant, sites in Madison within 2 km of each other and hosting very different gypsy moth densities also differed in whether pathogens were present.

EVALUATING THE PRACTICAL UTILITY OF HYPERSPECTRAL REMOTE SENSING IMAGERY: AN EAB CASE STUDY

Richard Hallett[1], Jennifer Pontius[1], Mary Martin[2], and Lucie Plourde[2]

[1]U.S. Forest Service, Northern Research Station, 271 Mast Rd., Durham, NH 03824

[2]Complex Systems Research Center,
University of New Hampshire, Morse Hall, Durham, NH 03824

ABSTRACT

The emerald ash borer (EAB) (*Agrilus planipennis*) is an exotic insect pest currently threatening ash species in the Great Lakes region. Because of the potential impact to forests in this area, multiple government agencies are currently focusing their efforts on developing new technologies to detect, monitor, and control this insect. Previous work has shown that hyperspectral remote sensing technologies can map detailed forest health and species abundance across large areas (Pontius et al. 2005a, b). This study examines the capability of a commercially available sensor (SPECTIR VNIR) to map ash decline in Michigan and Ohio (Fig. 1).

Specifically, our objectives were to:

1. Develop a field decline rating system that would capture and summarize the range of ash decline symptoms resulting from EAB infestation, including pre-visual symptoms

2. Locate and measure ground control plots covering a range of ash abundance and health

3. Use hyperspectral remote sensing imagery to predict decline on a landscape scale

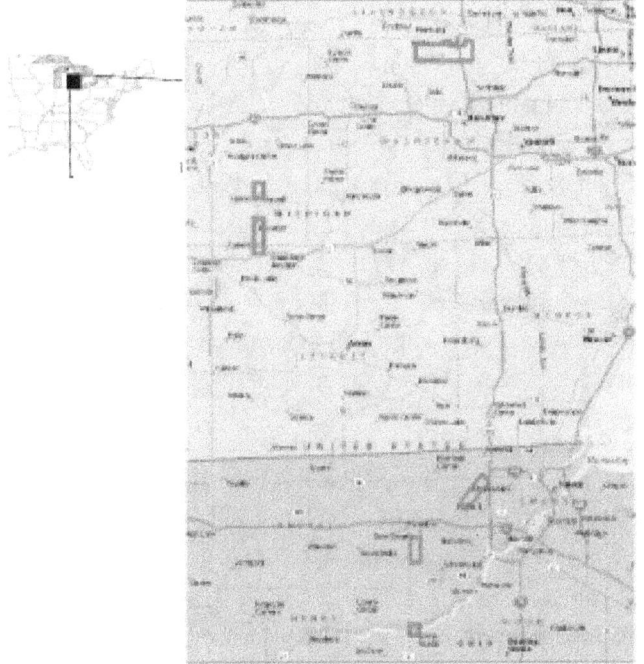

Figure 1. Six regions across southern MICHIGAN and northern OHIO were flown by a SPECTIR VNIR sensor for collection of high spatial resolution hyperspectral imagery. These regions cover a range of ash density, health, and EAB infestation levels.

Remote Sensing Imagery

On June 6, 2006, a SPECTIR VNIR sensor was flown on a fixed wing aircraft. This resulted in a 1-m resolution data collection over sections of Michigan and Ohio (Fig. 1), covering a range of EAB infestation and ash conditions. The resulting imagery covers 30,000 acres, with a spectral range of approximately 450 nm to 990 nm. SPECTIR delivered a Level 1 product, which included radiometrically calibrated, geometrically corrected flight lines. Other than applying a supplied INS correction to account for aircraft geometry, no additional pre-processing of the imagery was conducted. An ARC GIS shape file of all subject trees was used to extract spectra for calibration development on a pixel by pixel basis using ENVI (version 4.3) software.

Field Data Collection

Ground truth data for image calibration and validation were collected coincident with image acquisition from

28 10-factor prism plots in Michigan and Ohio. At each plot, all trees were individually mapped and geo-located using a Trimble GPS for direct comparison to the correct pixels within the imagery. This resulted in 60 dominant or co-dominant ash trees for foliage sampling and decline assessments. Foliage was collected from the middle and upper canopies of each tree using a 12-gauge shotgun. This sampling technique allowed us to efficiently target multiple sun-lit branches for collection from mature trees that are otherwise inaccessible.

Ash Decline Assessment

A summary decline value was quantified for each tree using methods specifically designed to capture the various, sequential symptoms that follow EAB infestation. This included several measurements commonly used in forest health assessment (vigor class, transparency, dieback, and live crown ratio), early stress symptoms (chlorophyll fluorescence indices), and symptoms specific to EAB infestation (woodpecker activity, epicormic branching, and exit hole counts).

A six-term linear regression equation based on known stress and chlorophyll sensitive indices was able to predict a 0 to 10 continuous decline rating scale (0=healthy, 10 = dead) with an $R^2 = 0.71$ and an average jackknifed residual of 0.61 (Fig. 2). Decline was predicted to within one class with 97% accuracy.

The ability of this instrument to assess decline below 4 (when dieback and transparency reach levels first noticeable in the field) is based upon pre-visual changes in chlorophyll that are characteristic of early stress (Fig. 3) (Carter and Miller 1994, Gitelson et al. 1996, Vogelmann et al. 1993).

While this decline prediction is not stressor- or species-specific, it will enable land managers to assess and monitor detailed changes in forest health across the landscape. Figure 4 is an example of the type of data product that can be produced using a combination of hyperspectral imagery and field calibration plots. Areas of incipient decline can be clearly seen and targeted for intensive examination by field crews.

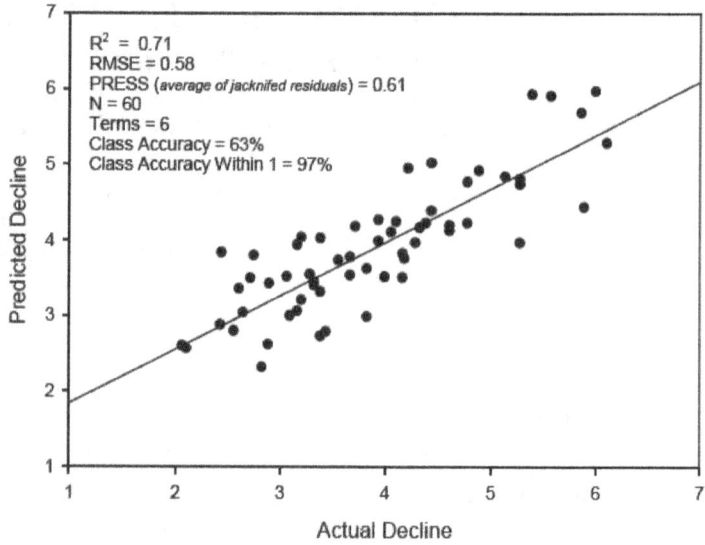

Figure 2. A six-term linear regression model based on chlorophyll and water sensitive indices was able to predict a detailed decline rating for ash with a one-class tolerance accuracy of 97%.

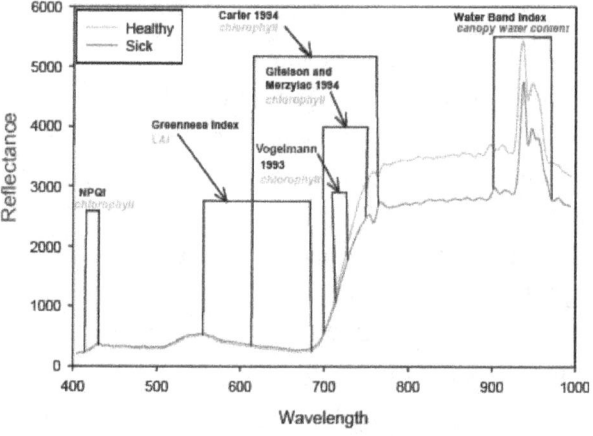

Figure 3. The full visible and NIR spectrum are not required to predict ash decline. Here we used six known plant stress indices that are sensitive to changes in chlorophyll content, function or canopy water content. Such indices generally pair a stress sensitive wavelength, with an insensitive wavelength to account for differences in shading, view angle, or background interferences.

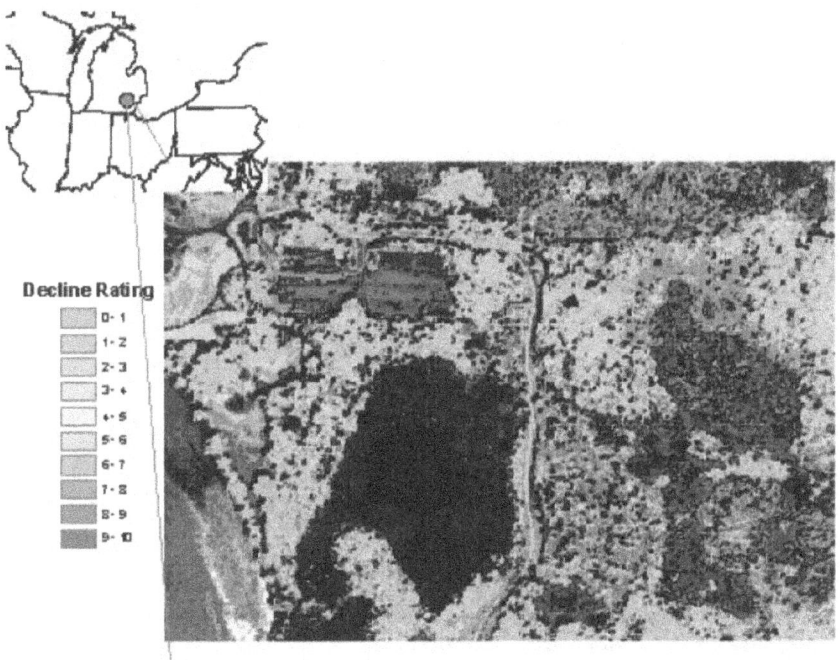

Figure 4. The predicted decline at Independence Lake, MI, a region of high ash density and prolonged EAB infestation, highlights large areas of severe decline. Average forest decline was 4.9 on the 0 to 10 scale (0= healthy, 10 = dead).

Ideally, healthy ash stands would be monitored yearly using these techniques in order to identify trees with degrading health. The early identification of infested areas would ensure that integrated pest management programs could be effectively implemented to better contain the spread of this insect.

Literature Cited

Carter, G.A.; Miller, R.L. 1994. **Early detection of plant stress by digital imaging within narrow stress-sensitive wavebands.** Remote Sensing of Environment. 50: 295-302.

Gitelson, A.A.; Merzlyak, M.N.; Lichtenthaler, H.K. 1996. **Detection of red edge position and chlorophyll content by reflectance measurements near 700 N m.** Journal of Plant Physiology. 148: 501-508.

Pontius, J.; Hallett, R.; Martin, M. 2005a. **Using AVIRIS to assess hemlock abundance and early decline in the Catskills, New York.** Remote Sensing of Environment. 97: 163-173.

Pontius, J.A.; Martin, M.E.; Plourde, L.; Hallett, R.A. 2005b. **Using hyperspectral technologies to map hemlock decline: pre-visual decline assessment for early infestation detection.** In: Proceedings of the hemlock woolly adelgid symposium. Asheville, NC. U.S. Forest Service, Morgantown, WV: 73-86.

Vogelmann, J.E.; Rock, B.N.; Moss, D.M. 1993. **Red edge spectral measurements from sugar maple leaves. International Journal of Remote Sensing. 14: 1563-1575.**

INVASIVE PLANTS IN THE GORDON NATURAL AREA: INFLUENCE OF PAST LAND USE ON COVER OF SELECTED INVASIVES

Gerard Hertel and Greg Turner

**Department of Biology, West Chester University of Pennsylvania
West Chester, PA 19383**

ABSTRACT

The 150-acre Robert G. Gordon Natural Area (GNA) on the campus of West Chester University was dedicated in 1973 for education, research, and protection of biodiversity. During 2002-2003, 18 forest health monitoring (FHM) plots, each composed of four (24- ft- radius) subplots, were established at the GNA following protocols developed by the U.S. Forest Service. Vegetation was surveyed in the plots to evaluate how land use history affects the colonization and success of the four most common invasive exotic species. Initially, only exotic trees were measured, but all vegetation was measured in 2004. Each exotic species was recorded, and cover (0-2, 2 to 6, 6 to 16, and 16+ft) was estimated for those species greater than 1% cover. FHM plots were classified to represent five past land use history categories: (1) old farm field; (2) floodplain; (3) large forest fragment; (4) small forest fragment; and (5) old orchard. The four invasive exotic species were Norway maple (*Acer platanoides* L.), tree-of-heaven (*Ailanthus altissima* (Mill.) Swingle), Japanese stilt grass (*Microstegium vimineum* (Trin.) *A. Camus*), and Japanese honeysuckle (*Lonicera japonica* Thunb.). Norway maple dominated the orchard and large forest fragment, Japanese stilt grass dominated the floodplain, Japanese honeysuckle dominated the old farm field, and tree-of-heaven dominated the small forest fragment, suggesting that different land uses may influence exotic presence after regeneration. While habitat canopies were dominated by native species, dramatic reductions in abundance by most native understory trees since 1970, and arrival by invasive exotic species across habitats (and deer), suggest that forest composition will change at the GNA to include more beech and white ash, but fewer tuliptree, hickories, and oaks. Exotic species will dramatically increase in abundance unless their recruitment is managed.

IMPACT OF KUDZU ON SOIL NITROGEN AND SOIL MICROBIAL COMMUNITIES

Jonathan E. Hickman and Manuel Lerdau

State University of New York, Stony Brook, NY 11794

ABSTRACT

Kudzu (*Pueraria montana*), a leguminous vine native to Asia, covers more than 3 million ha in the southeastern United States and is expanding its range northward. With its high rates of nitrogen fixation in its native range and high degree of nodulation and nitrogenase activity in the United States, kudzu is likely to present a substantial new source of nitrogen to these ecosystems. To date, however, the impacts of kudzu invasion on nitrogen cycling in the eastern United States have not been investigated. We examined kudzu's effect on nitrogen inputs to soil and nitrogen cycling at three pairs of invaded and uninvaded sites in Maryland. Newly senesced litter from kudzu contains significantly higher concentrations of nitrogen than that of co-occurring tree species, suggesting that kudzu represents a new source of organic nitrogen in these sites. Inorganic nitrogen in soils bears out this suggestion: nitrate levels were four times higher in sites invaded by kudzu in April 2006 and remained higher throughout the growing season. We also found increases and trends toward increases in rates of nitrification, nitrogen mineralization, and denitrification enzyme activity in September 2005 although these patterns were not maintained in early 2006. Overall, our data strongly suggest that kudzu is having significant impacts on the nitrogen cycling and availability of invaded ecosystems.

MOLECULAR IDENTIFICATION OF ECTOMYCORRHIZAL FUNGI ASSOCIATED WITH THE AMERICAN CHESTNUT

Shiv Hiremath and Kirsten Lehtoma

U.S. Forest Service, Northern Research Station
359 Main Rd., Delaware, OH 43015

ABSTRACT

We plan to use American chestnut trees for reforesting reclaimed mine sites in southeastern Ohio. The American chestnut was once common to this region but was displaced because of the blight-causing invasive fungus *Cryphonectria parasitica*. However, with increased efforts to generate blight-resistant varieties of the American chestnut through breeding programs as well as use of hypovirulent strains of the fungus that can provide resistance to the trees, restoration of the American chestnut now appears feasible. Our approach to using chestnut seedlings for reforestation addresses both issues: (1) reclamation of mined lands and (2) restoration of the American chestnut.

Mycorrhizal fungi can significantly aid in reforestation efforts because the fungi can offer many benefits for the survival and healthy growth of the planted seedlings in the nutrient-poor mined sites. While there have been many reports of association of mycorrhizal fungi with the American chestnut, systematic studies to identify species that form functional symbiotic interactions with chestnut tree roots and their utility in chestnut restoration efforts have not been carried out. The traditional methods of identifying the associated fungi using morphological techniques are often inconclusive or not precise. We are using molecular detection methods coupled with transmission electron microscope (TEM) analyses to identify functional associations of ectomycorrhizal fungi with the roots of chestnut seedlings.

The seedlings were inoculated under semi-sterile conditions in the laboratory, and mycorrhizal formation was allowed to progress in the greenhouse. After 3 months, roots were examined under a dissecting microscope for the presence of the micorrhiza. The mycorrhizal tissues were also subjected to TEM analysis to confirm symbiotic interaction. The tissue was then used for DNA extraction and for analyses. Identification of ectomycorrhizal fungal species was achieved through comparison of ribosomal DNA internal transcribed spacer (ITS) sequences with those deposited in public databases. Among the several pairs of primers suggested for these analyses, the following pairs were used: (ITS-1 – LR21) and (ITS-1 – ITS-4). We were able to identify and confirm that the following inoculated fungi can successfully form associations with American chestnut seedlings. They were *Cenococcum geophilum*, *Amanita rubescens*, *Laccaria bicolor*, *Pisolithus tinctorius*, and *Laccaria laccata*. In addition, we also identified two fungi that were not used in inoculation experiments. These were probably associated with the chestnut seeds before their germination. The molecular technique identified them as *Thelephora terrestris* and *Tometella* sp. We are generating and planting seedlings inoculated with these fungi in reclaimed regions and monitoring their survival and growth.

TWO APPROACHES FOR QUANTIFYING TRANSMISSION OF MICROSPORIDIA IN SEMI-FIELD CONDITIONS

Gernot Hoch[1], Vincent D'Amico[2], Leellen F. Solter[3], Milan Zubrik[4], and Michael L. McManus[5]

[1] BOKU – University of Natural Resources, Vienna, Austria

[2] U.S. Forest Service, Northern Research Station/ University of Delaware, Townsend Hall, Newark, DE 19717

[3] Illinois Natural History Survey, 1816 S. Oak St., Champaign, IL 61820

[4] Forest Research Institute Zvolen, Lesnicka 11, 96923 Banska Stiavnica, Slovak Republic

[5] U.S. Forest Service, Northern Research Station, 51 Mill Pond Rd., Hamden, CT 06514

ABSTRACT

Horizontal transmission of the microsporidium *Nosema lymantriae* in *Lymantria dispar* larvae in semi-field conditions was quantified using two approaches: we varied (1) the density of the pathogen and (2) the time that susceptible larvae were exposed. Wood-framed cages were installed around fifteen 2-m-tall *Quercus petraea* trees on an oak plantation. Different trees were used each year. To study transmission at different pathogen densities, *L. dispar* larvae that were inoculated and marked in the laboratory (= inoculated larvae) and uninfected, susceptible larvae (= test larvae) were placed in the cages in ratios of 10:90, 20:80, 30:70, 40:60, and 50:50 larvae, respectively. All larvae were removed from the cage after 21 days. Two trials in consecutive years were conducted. To test transmission at different times of exposure, 30 marked, inoculated larvae and 70 test larvae were placed into the cage at the same time. Larvae were removed from the cages at three points in time: 11, 16, and 21 days of exposure.

Transmission at Different Pathogen Densities

The number of inoculated larvae affected prevalence of infections in test larvae. The prevalence was variable, but there were no differences between the two trials.

Moreover, there was no significant interaction between trials and number of inoculated larvae. Infection of test larvae increased with increasing numbers of inoculated larvae (from $14.2\pm3.5\%$ at density of 10 inoculated larvae to $36.7\pm5.7\%$ at 30 inoculated larvae). At higher densities, percent infection in test larvae appeared to level off ($35.7\pm5.5\%$ at 50 inoculated larvae). A logarithmic function best fit to our data ($R^2=0.330$, $F=13.783$, $P<0.001$).

Transmission at Different Times of Exposure

No transmission of *Nosema* infections occurred within the first 15 days post inoculation (11 days of exposure). Transmission increased over time; we found the first infected test larvae in samples taken 20 dpi (16 days of exposure). In the cages sampled 25 dpi (21 days of exposure), *Nosema* prevalence in test larvae ranged from 20.6 to 39.2%. The results of our experiments show that *N. lymantriae* is efficiently transmitted under field conditions. Data from concurrent laboratory studies suggest that this is mainly due to spores that are released via feces. Increasing transmission with increasing time of exposure reflects the increasing pathogen density due to this release of spores from living larvae.

BIOLOGICAL CONTROL OF MILE-A-MINUTE WEED

Judith A. Hough-Goldstein

Department of Entomology and Wildlife Ecology, University of Delaware, Newark DE 19716-2160

ABSTRACT

Mile-a-minute weed (*Polygonum perfoliatum* L.) is an alien invasive weed from Asia that infests natural areas in a variety of habitats. This annual vine is a prolific seed producer and has become a serious problem in the mid-Atlantic region. The North American population is thought to have originated near York, PA, in the 1930s, probably accidentally introduced with holly seed imported from Japan (Moul 1948). Although it was recognized as a potentially dangerous weed that should be eradicated, no action was taken, and the weed can now be found from Delaware west to Ohio, south to West Virginia, and north to Massachusetts. A biological control program was initiated by the U.S. Forest Service in 1996. Over 100 insect species were identified on mile-a-minute weed in China, including several that appeared to have a narrow host-range (Ding et al. 2004). One of these, *Rhinoncomimus latipes* Korotyaev 1997, was tested on plant species in China and in quarantine in Delaware, and found to be extremely host-specific (Colpetzer et al. 2004). This insect was approved by APHIS for release in 2004.

Eggs of *R. latipes* are laid on plants and hatch in about 5 days. Neonates crawl along stems and enter a node, where they feed internally for about 1-2 weeks, after which they drop out of the stem and pupate in the soil. Adults emerge about 1 week later and feed on mile-a-minute weed leaves and terminals. The weevils have been reared at the N.J. Dept. of Agriculture Phillip Alampi Beneficial Insect Laboratory since fall of 2004, and in 2006 more than 20,000 weevils were reared and released. Most releases have occurred in New Jersey, but insects have also been released and have established in sites in Delaware, Pennsylvania, West Virginia, and Maryland. Although it is too soon to assess their impact in the field, plant mortality has been observed in some areas where weevils have heavily defoliated mile-a-minute weed plants in New Jersey.

The impact of the weevil on *P. perfoliatum* seed production was assessed on single plants in replicated field cages (N=6 per treatment) in 2006, with two levels of weevil numbers (5 or 20 per cage) added at two different times (May 26 or June 23); plants in cages with no weevils were included as a control. Seed production was almost completely suppressed between late July and mid-September in the cages with early application of weevils, both low and high levels; however, all plants produced numerous seeds in October, resulting in no significant difference by treatment in total seed production over the season. In this experiment the caged plants were unusually large and robust because of minimal competition with other plants. The experiment will be repeated in 2007 with the addition of more natural levels of plant competition, which should lead to greater impact by the herbivore.

In summary, *R. latipes* can be successfully laboratory reared, and the weevils have been shown to establish well in a variety of field situations. Multiple, overlapping generations occur during the season, and there are indications of plant mortality in the field where heavy defoliation has been observed. A preliminary cage study showed a definite impact of weevil feeding on the phenology of seed production by individual plants, but without the stress of competition, caged plants survived and produced large numbers of seeds even with substantial weevil damage.

Literature Cited

Colpetzer, K.; Hough-Goldstein, J.; Ding, J.; Fu, W. 2004. **Host specificity of the Asian weevil, *Rhinoncomimus latipes* Korotyaev (Coleoptera: Curculionidae), a potential biological control agent of mile-a-minute weed, *Polygonum perfoliatum* L. (*Polygonales: Polygonaceae*).** Biological Control. 30: 511-522.

Ding, J.; Fu, W.; Reardon, R.; Wu, Y.; Zhang, G. 2004. **Exploratory survey in China for potential insect biocontrol agents of mile-a-minute weed, *Polygonum perfoliatum* L., in eastern USA.** Biological Control. 30: 487-495.

Moul, E.T. 1948. **A dangerous weedy *Polygonum* in Pennsylvania.** Rhodora. 50: 64-66.

SPATIOTEMPORAL DYNAMICS OF INVASIVE BARK BEETLES: MODELING DISPERSAL STRATEGIES

Kyrre Kausrud[1], Bjørn Økland[2], Olav Skarpaas[3], Nils Chr. Stenseth[1], and Nadir Erbilgin[4]

[1]Centre for Ecological and Evolutionary Synthesis, Box 1050 Blindern, N-0316, Oslo, Norway

[2]Norwegian Forest and Landscape Institute, Box 115, N-1431 Ås, Norway

[3]Norwegian Institute for Nature Research, Gaustadalléen 21, NO-0349 Oslo, Norway

[4]Division of Organisms and Environment, University of California, Berkeley, CA 94720

ABSTRACT

Extensive timber imports represent potential introduction pathways for exotic bark beetles (Col: Scolytidae) that may pose ecological hazards and economical risks to native forests. One such species, *Ips amitinus* Eichh., has been intercepted several times at Norwegian ports of entry in the years since 2002, the year of the first Scandinavian record. Detection of overwintering individuals of *I. amitinus* at the timber storage site of import timber and preliminary results of a stepwise import model may suggest a high risk of establishment and spread in Norway spruce forests in Scandinavia.

Using various modeling approaches, our goal is to reduce the risk of introduction, establishment, and spread of introduced bark beetles. Our objectives are to (1) model the processes of dispersal and establishment of arriving bark beetles; (2) explore to what extent an introduced species interacting with native *Ips typographus* L., the most dominant species in Norway spruce, will lead to stronger and more frequent outbreaks of *I. typographus*; (3) assess potential patterns of spread of newly established bark beetle species and the spatiotemporal outbreak dynamics resulting from interactions between native and introduced species; and (4) advise on the implications for forest industry and management.

Here we present current efforts to model dispersal (objective 1). Dispersal patterns, and hence rates of establishment and spread, may vary considerably depending on dispersal behaviors of insects, such as directionality of movement and aggregation propensity. To assess underlying assumptions of dispersal models, we are using an individual-based model where traits governing dispersal are inherited with random mutations. Individual reproductive success is determined by resource availability and density-dependence in a simulated landscape governed by external forces (e.g., windfellings) and beetle activity (consumption of resources). Evolvable traits include straight line vs. random-walk flight paths and aggregation propensity. Model simulations show that the chance of successful reproduction is greatest for intermediate to high levels of directionality, and that directionality increases over time up to a certain point determined by the landscape features as well as other traits of the species. Assuming limited (local) information in a stochastic landscape, intermediate to high degree of flight directionality is selected for.

HOW LONG DOES IT TAKE TENERAL ADULT ASIAN LONGHORNED BEETLES TO SCLERITIZE AND THEN CHEW OUT OF THE WOOD?

Melody A. Keena and Vicente Sánchez

U.S. Forest Service, Northern Research Station, Northeastern Center for Forest Health Research, Hamden, CT 06514-1703

ABSTRACT

The Asian longhorned beetle (*Anoplophora glabripennis* (Motschulsky)) (Coleoptera: Cerambycidae) is an introduced invasive pest with the potential to devastate hardwood forests (especially *Acer*-dominated forests) in North America. Information on the basic biology of this beetle is critical for providing the biological basis for predicting phenology that can be used to time exclusion and eradication methodologies. Using artificial pupal chambers, we documented the amount of time required by teneral adults at three temperatures (20, 25, and 30 °C), 60-80%RH, and 16:8 light: dark photoperiod to scleritize after eclosion and subsequently chew out through a plug of Norway maple wood. In the study, we used 218 laboratory-reared pupae (within a few days of eclosion) from the Chicago, IL, or Inner Mongolia, China, strains.

The average depth of wood that the beetles chewed through was 7 mm (range 3-11 mm). Females (1.54 ± 0.03 g) weighed significantly more than males (1.12 ± 0.03 g), but the average weights of the beetles emerging at each temperature did not differ. Adult weight was positively correlated with exit hole diameter (diam. = 2.2 * weight (g) + 7.9). The rate at which beetles chewed through the wood (136, 178, and 168 mm/d at 20, 25, and 30 °C, respectively) significantly differed between temperatures. Heavier adults did not chew significantly faster than lighter adults although that was the trend. Temperature has a significant effect on the time it takes adults to scleritize and chew through Norway maple wood. On average, it took 7, 5, and 4 days to scleritize and 5, 4, and 4 days to chew out at 20, 25, and 30 °C, respectively, suggesting that beetles spend more than a week in the wood even at summer temperatures. These results can be used in a variety of ways to better define beetle behavior and population dynamics.

DOUGLAS-FIR AS A NEW HOST PLANT FOR SIBERIAN MOTH–A POTENTIAL INVADER

Nataliya I. Kirichenko[1], Yuri N. Baranchikov[1], and Stefan Vidal[2]

[1]V.N. Sukachev Institute of Forest, Siberian Branch, Russian Academy of Science
50 Akademgorodok, Krasnoyarsk 660039, Russia

[2]Department of Crop Sciences, Entomological Section, Georg-August University,
Grisebachstr., 6, D-37077 Goettingen, Germany

ABSTRACT

The Siberian moth (SM) (*Dendrolimus superans sibiricus* Tschetv.) (Lepidoptera, Lasiocampidae) is the most destructive pest of conifers in Northern Asia. The risk of this species occurring in North America is considered high. In an assessment for potential import of larch logs from Russia into the U.S., this species was identified as a potential hitchhiker with a medium likelihood of being associated with the host on any shipment with high transport potential. Northern U.S. states and Canada have an appropriate climate and are forested with conifers that may be suitable for establishment of the pest. Nevertheless, the favorability of North American coniferous species for the SM has not been determined yet.

We checked experimentally if *Pseudotsuga menziesii* (Pm.) or Douglas-fir (not native for natural SM habitats) can serve as a potential host plant for SM larvae. We also compared the suitability of Douglas-fir and larch (*Larix decidua* (Ledeb.) for the pest larvae performance.

The work was done at the quarantine facility of Georg-August University (Goettingen) on I-VI instar larvae of SM originated from the Republic of Tuva, Russia. Foliage of European larch and Douglas-fir were collected daily from a nearby arboretum. Foliage was fed to individually reared larvae kept under constant conditions: 24 hours illumination, 20-22°C, and 60% relative humidity. Host preference of the first-instar larvae was determined in two-choice tests as a number of larvae found on each host after 1 hour from experiment set; 10 larvae per Petri dish in 20 replications.

European larch was found to be a highly suitable host for the SM larva; this agrees with results obtained earlier for SM in its natural habitats in Siberia and the Russian Far East. Douglas-fir appeared to be a similarly suitable host plant: no differences were found in survival and growth rates of I-VI instar larvae of SM reared on the tested plant species. Larch needles were preferred slightly more by neonate larvae in the two-choice tests.

This work was supported by Deutscher Akademischer Austauschdienst, Germany and Krasnoyarsk Regional Scientific Fund, Russia.

DEVELOPMENT OF NOVEL ASH HYBRIDS TO INTROGRESS EMERALD ASH BORER RESISTANCE INTO NORTH AMERICAN ASH SPECIES

Jennifer Koch[1], Mary Mason[2], Alieta Eyles[3], David Carey[1], Richard Larson[4], Charlotte Chan[5], David Smitley[6], Pierluigi Bonello[3], and Dan Herms[2]

[1]U.S. Forest Service, Northern Research Station, 359 Main Rd., Delaware, OH 43015

[2]The Ohio State University, Department of Entomology, Ohio Agricultural Research and Development Center, 1680 Madison Ave., Wooster, OH 44691

[3]The Ohio State University, Department of Plant Pathology, 2021 Coffey Rd., Columbus, OH 43210

[4]Dawes Arboretum, 7770 Jacksontown Rd., Newark, OH 43056

[5]The Holden Arboretum, 9717 Mitchell's Mill Rd., Kirtland, OH 44094

[6]Michigan State University, Department of Entomology, 347 Natural Science, East Lansing, MI 48824

ABSTRACT

The emerald ash borer (EAB) (*Agrilus planipennis* Fairmaire) is a beetle native to Asia that has been introduced into the Great Lakes region, where it is rapidly spreading. EAB larvae feed under the bark, destroying cambium and phloem tissues, and causing mortality of mature trees in 3-4 years. Currently, no resistance has been identified in native North American ash species, putting the entire ash resource of the eastern U.S. and Canada at risk of loss due to EAB. In contrast to the rapid destruction of ash trees in the United States by EAB, outbreaks of EAB in Asia appear to be isolated responses to stress and do not devastate the ash population. It is likely that heritable genetic resistance to EAB is part of the reason EAB damage is less severe in Asia.

In 2005, a Joint Venture Agreement was initiated between the U.S. Forest Service and The Ohio State University. The Dawes Arboretum and the Holden Arboretum are also actively involved in this multi-organization effort. The goal of this collaboration is to identify ash species that are resistant to EAB, identify the underlying molecular mechanisms of resistance, and use this knowledge to develop a breeding program to introgress EAB resistance into North American ash species. To date, common garden studies have indicated that *Fraxinus mandshurica* has some level of EAB resistance and several other European and Asian species are currently being tested. Comparisons of phloem extracts from *F. americana*, *F. pennsylvanica*, and *F. mandshurica* demonstrate both qualitative and quantitative differences that may, in part, explain the enhanced resistance of *F. mandshurica*. Biochemical approaches, including protein analysis, continue to be used to uncover the mechanisms involved in EAB resistance. Two years of breeding efforts have produced a few putative interspecific hybrids including two progeny from a *F. chinensis* x *F. americana* cross, and six progeny from a *F. excelsior* x *F. pennsylvanica* cross. The phenotypes of these trees are under evaluation and marker studies are being used to confirm their hybrid parentage. Many barriers to successful hybridization exist including interspecies differences in ploidy levels, pollination mechanisms, and reproductive biology. Methods of overcoming these barriers are being developed.

DISPERSAL AND IMPACT OF THE MILE-A-MINUTE WEEVIL: A TWO-YEAR STUDY IN SOUTHEASTERN PENNSYLVANIA

Ellen C. Lake and Judith A. Hough-Goldstein

Department of Entomology and Wildlife Ecology, University of Delaware
250 Townsend Hall, Newark, DE 19716

ABSTRACT

Mile-a-minute weed (*Polygonum perfoliatum*) was introduced to the United States in the late 1930s and has spread to 11 states ranging from Massachusetts to West Virginia. Mile-a-minute germinates early in the spring, outcompetes other plants in a variety of habitats, and seeds prolifically. The USDA approved the release of the curculionid weevil Rhinoncomimus latipes Korotyaev, the mile-a-minute weevil, for biological control of this annual invasive weed in 2004. Weevil adults feed on mile-a-minute foliage; the larvae feed within nodes and may cause sufficient damage to reduce seed production. The weevils are active from early spring through multiple hard frosts in the fall and complete at least four generations. Weevils have been released in Delaware, Maryland, New Jersey, Pennsylvania, and West Virginia and have established at every release site.

Three 50-m-diameter release arrays in southeastern Pennsylvania were monitored to track weevil dispersal and impact on mile-a-minute. The weevils established at all release sites and populations increased in 2006 compared to 2005. Within 14 months, weevils had dispersed to mile-a-minute patches up to 800 m from the release. Seed cluster production was lower in 2006 than in 2005 at all three Pennsylvania sites and at several New Jersey release sites. The ability to establish populations, coupled with a high reproductive rate and dispersal capacity, bodes well for the potential of the weevil to be an effective biological control agent for mile-a-minute. Further research is needed to learn more about the weevil's efficacy as a control agent and about the best methods to conduct releases and incorporate the weevils into an integrated weed management program.

THE EXOTIC BANDED ELM BARK BEETLE AND THE SMALLER EUROPEAN ELM BARK BEETLE: ABUNDANCE AND HOST ATTRACTION

Jana C. Lee[1], Shakeeb Hamud[2], Jose Negron[3], Jeff Witcosky[4], A. Steve Munson[5], and Steven J. Seybold[2]

[1]Department of Entomology, University of California–Davis, One Shields Avenue, Davis, CA 95616

[2]U.S. Forest Service, Pacific Southwest Research Station, 720 Olive Dr, Suite D, Davis, CA 95616

[3]U.S. Forest Service, Rocky Mountain Research Station, 240 West Prospect Rd., Ft. Collins, CO 80526-2098

[4]U.S. Forest Service, Region 2, Forest Health Protection, P.O. Box 25127, Lakewood, CO 80225

[5]U.S. Forest Service, Region 4, Forest Health Protection, 4746 S. 1900 E. Ogden, UT 84403

ABSTRACT

In April 2003, the banded elm bark beetle (BEBB) (*Scolytus schevyrewi* Semenov), an invasive from Asia, was first detected in North America in Colorado and Utah. To date, BEBB has been detected in 21 states. BEBB attacks elm trees (*Ulmus* spp.) and may potentially vector the fungal pathogen causing Dutch elm disease. BEBB shares a similar biology and appearance with an established invasive, the European elm bark beetle (EEBB) (*Scolytus multistriatus* (Marsham)). However, BEBB seems to attack standing trees more aggressively and appears now more abundant than EEBB in the Rocky Mountain region, suggesting that it may have displaced EEBB and/or is better able to colonize regions beyond EEBB's range. Our objectives were to determine the relative abundance of BEBB and EEBB in California, Nevada, Utah, Colorado, and Utah.

A trap Siberian elm log, baited funnel trap, and passive plexiglass Schmidt trap were set up at four sites in each state and monitored from May to September. BEBB was far less common than EEBB in California (12% = 100*BEBB/ (BEBB+EEBB)), and BEBB increased in abundance from Nevada (43%), Utah (60%), and Colorado and Wyoming (90%). The attraction of BEBB and EEBB to hosts American elm (*U. Americana*) and Siberian elm (*U. pumila*) and the same hosts infested with conspecifics were tested with flight traps baited with uninfested and infested bolts.

In Colorado and Wyoming, BEBB was very attracted to Siberian elms bolts alone or infested with conspecifics. This suggests that BEBB is responding to host and not pheromonal cues during the initial stages of infestation. In California, EEBB was most attracted to Siberian elm bolts infested with other EEBB, and attracted to a lesser degree to uninfested Siberian elm bolts. This suggests that EEBB was responding to host cues, and even more to pheromonal cues. Both BEBB and EEBB were less attracted to American than Siberian elm bolts, which could indicate a preference. However, we suspect this difference was due to the lower quality of the American elm sample in which the phloem was noticeably less moist.

DISTRIBUTION PATTERNS OF IMIDACLOPRID IN SAPLINGS AND LARGE TREES

Phillip A. Lewis, Molly M. Botts, and John J. Molongoski

USDA Animal and Plant Health Inspection Service, Pest Survey, Detection and
Exclusion Laboratory, Otis Air National Guard Base, MA 02542

ABSTRACT

Eradication of Asian longhorned beetle (*Anoplophora glabripennis*) populations in the United States is reliant on effective applications of the systemic insecticide imidacloprid. Most of the applications are made by low-pressure soil injection of a concentrated solution directed at the base of the tree. This study looked at imidacloprid distribution in saplings of elm, green ash, red and silver maple, and several shade trees growing in a cemetery.

Greenhouse Study

Dormant saplings were soaked in a 20-ppm imidacloprid solution for 4 days (100 mL/sapling) and then individually potted along with any remaining solution. After leaf-out, plants were variously dissected and compared. One group compared whole plant extractions of the four plant species, a second divided plants into aboveground and belowground portions, and a third compared residue present within stems to leaves of the same plant.

The significantly higher imidacloprid residue levels seen in silver maple saplings compared with the other three species in the greenhouse study may be due to a difference in the physiology of trees of this species that allows them to take up more imidacloprid or to take it up more quickly as they break dormancy. The generally higher pesticide residues found in the roots compared with that in the leaves + stems of Group 1 plants may be an indication that the saplings were not given sufficient time to leaf out so that the pesticide could fully translocate.

Future investigations will look at sampling several trees over an interval of time to determine whether imidacloprid levels in roots drop off with a corresponding increase in leaf residues. Significantly higher residues seen in leaves compared with stems are probably due to the general translocation of materials to younger and growing tissues. This was observed with imidacloprid in a study by Mendel et al. on xylem transport in citrus (Acta Hort. 531, pp. 129-134). Our recent studies have found that residues in twigs were about six to seven times lower than that seen in leaves.

Shade Tree Study

Four 10- to 12-inch d.b.h. Norway maple trees were treated by trunk injection with imidacloprid and intensively sampled 3 months after treatment. Twelve samples per tree were taken at three heights--low, middle, and upper canopy—and from each cardinal direction.

There was no significant effect on imidacloprid residue levels due to sampling from different heights or sides of a tree, which justifies ground-based sampling with pole pruners. Residue levels varied greatly within a tree. The largest range between two sampling points in a tree was about 400 ppm. The high variation suggests that a large number of small samples can be taken from multiple points throughout the lower half of the canopy to best reflect the imidacloprid level present in a particular tree.

AERIAL APPLICATION OF SPINOSAD FOR EAB CONTROL IN WOODLOTS

Phillip A. Lewis[1], David Smitley[2], Richard Reardon[3], and Victor C. Mastro[1]

[1]USDA Animal and Plant Health Inspection Service, Pest Survey, Detection and Exclusion Laboratory, Otis Air National Guard Base, MA 02542

[2]Deptartment of Entomology, Michigan State University, East Lansing, MI 48824

[3]U.S. Forest Service, Northern Research Station, 180 Canfield St., Morgantown, WV 26505-3180

ABSTRACT

One of the pressing needs for effective management of the emerald ash borer (*Agrilus planipennis* Fairmaire) is an insecticide that can be used over large, wooded acreages where this insect has been identified as recently introduced or where it is found in low population numbers. Spinosad is a biological insecticide produced by a soil bacterium that has been shown to be toxic to the adult life stage of the EAB and is a superior candidate for use in aerial applications.

Spinosad is in common use by organic growers and was granted a "Green Chemistry" award by the U.S. Environmental Protection Agency, which classifies it as "reduced risk" because of its good environmental profile. It is moderately to slightly toxic to most fish and aquatic invertebrates, practically non-toxic to avian and mammalian species, and practically non-toxic to many beneficial insects. Spinosad has short half-lives in soil (9-17 days), on foliage (4-16 days), and in water (hours to 2 days) and has very low potential for runoff or leaching because it binds strongly to soil.

A test application of spinosad (GF-976, a formulation with 4 lb of active ingredient per gallon) was conducted on isolated woodlots surrounded by agricultural fields; woodlots were chosen that had apparent, low levels of EAB infestation. The six treatment and six control lots ranged in size from 8 to 30 acres and were located in Shiawassee County, Michigan. Two applications were made on June 13 and 27 at a rate of 7.2 oz of product in a ½ gallon of water per acre. Rotary atomizers were used and the VMD ranged from 130 to 145 μ. A Section 18 "emergency exemption" registration was granted by the EPA for the application because the existing label did not allow for treatment against EAB or for an aerial application over forest stands.

The impact of the application on target and non-target insects was assessed and compared with results from the control plots. Foliage was collected for analysis of spinosad residue at regular intervals post-application. Twelve ash trees from each plot were felled 3-4 months post-application, and eight branches from the upper crown of each tree were collected and processed to assess the impact of the application on the larval population.

Dead adult EAB were found under treated ash trees in the woodlots up to 7 days post-application, with the number of adults collected declining over time. Treated foliage was collected from four treated plots and a control plot 1 day and 7 days post-application, and then exposed to adult EAB for 5 days in the laboratory. Mortality ranged from 50 to 100% for the newly treated foliage and 10 to 50% for field-aged foliage, which verifies that the insecticide is broken down over time. Preliminary information from insects collected in Malaise traps shows no demonstrable effect on non-target species as a result of the treatment (Fig. 1).

Ultimately, the efficacy of aerial applications of spinosad to suppress populations of EAB in woodlots must be evaluated by the density of galleries in the fall following treatment. The mean density ± SD of galleries in control woodlots was 6.0 ± 7.2 compared with 2.5 ± 4.2 in spinosad-sprayed woodlots. Although the mean density of galleries was reduced by 58% in treated woodlots, this difference was not significant in a statistical analysis, most likely due to considerable variation in the starting density of EAB in the test woodlots, and by having only six plots to compare for each treatment (Fig. 2).

Spinosad looks promising as an aerial application for suppressing EAB because drop cloth sampling and foliage bioassays indicate that spinosad was effective against adults. Overall, larval populations of EAB were reduced by 58% in treated woodlots, whereas no effect was observed on non-target insects. A second year of treatments to the same woodlots in 2007 should yield more accurate results because there will be a good estimate of the starting population before the 2007 treatment.

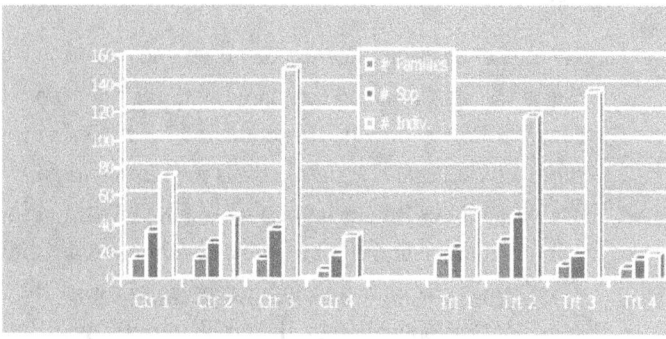

Figure 1. Insects caught from 0 to 2 days after application (Lepidoptera, Hymenoptera, Coleoptera).

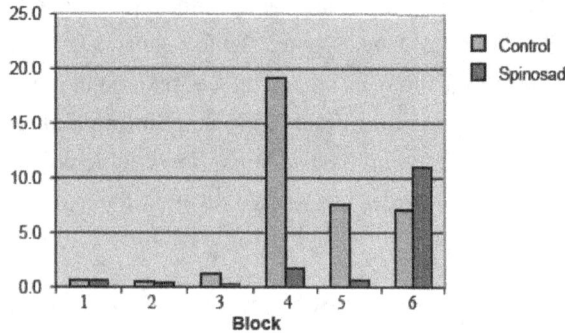

Figure 2. Larval population density (galleries/m^2) in control and treatment plots.

EXPLORING WAYS TO SERVE YOUR SCIENCE: PROVIDING FOREST THREAT INFORMATION TO A VARIETY OF AUDIENCES

Karin P. Lichtenstein, Bridget O'Hara, James F. Fox, Joe Brownsmith, April Pallette, Jeff Hicks, and J. Greg Dobson

National Environmental Modeling and Analysis Center, University of North Carolina Asheville, Rhoades 201 CPO#2345, Asheville, NC 28804

ABSTRACT

The Eastern Forest Environmental Threat Assessment Center (EFETAC) was established to generate, integrate, and apply knowledge in order to predict, detect, and assess environmental threats to public and private forests of the eastern U.S., and to deliver this knowledge to managers in ways that are timely, useful, and user friendly. The collaboration between EFETAC and the National Environmental Modeling and Analysis Center (NEMAC) aims to support this mission with the development of advanced tools and technologies that support integrated threat assessments for a variety of audiences.

These audiences are separated into three main categories based on their needs for data access related to Forest Threats. The three categories are (1) general public including land owners; (2) forest professionals including research scientists, forest managers, and extension specialists; and (3) decision makers, which includes all of these and policy makers.

The foundation of the Forest Threat Toolset is an integrated database system that will serve information to all of the data access tools. The four main threat assessment tools in development are (1) Forest Threat Summary Viewer, (2) Forest Threat GIS Viewer, (3) Forest Threat Search Tool, and (4) Comparative Risk Assessment Framework and Tool Version 2 (CRAFT V2).

These tools will (1) educate the public and land owners with useful online information and knowledge generated by the U.S. Forest Service and its partners about threats that are impacting their land; (2) provide rapid access to new, integrated, and relevant data and information for forest professionals, researchers, and scientists; and (3) deliver a superior team-facilitated decision making process that uses all technologies of the Forest Threat Toolset including GIS map-viewers, database systems, search engines, and Wiki technologies to make the most informed decisions about threats to our eastern forests.

The development of innovative, robust, and advanced technologies and tools, as well as the coordination of data sharing and communication among other EFETAC partnerships, will address the common recognition of the need for integrated threat assessments.

SUPPLEMENTAL FOOD PREFERENCE FOR THE WEAVER ANT, A POTENTIAL BIOLOGICAL CONTROL AGENT OF THE MAHOGANY SHOOT BORER

Grace T. Lim[1&2], Scott M. Salom[1], Loke T. Kok[1], and Laurence G. Kirton[2]

[1]Department of Entomology, Virginia Tech, 216A Price Hall MC0319, Blacksburg, VA 24061

[2]Forest Research Institute Malaysia, Entomology Section, Kepong, Selangor, 52109, Malaysia

ABSTRACT

Supplemental feeding is being investigated as a method to enhance the performance of the weaver ant (*Oecophylla smaragdina* Fabricius) (Hymenoptera: Formicidae), a promising biological control agent of the mahogany shoot borer (*Hypsipyla robusta*) (Lepidoptera: Pyralidae) in Malaysia. The nests of this aggressive, predatory tree-dwelling ant can be harvested from various host plant species and redistributed to mahogany plantations that need its protection. Choice and no-choice tests assessed the preference of ant colonies for four foods. In the choice test, six ant colonies were each provided ad libitum access to four food choices on a feeding platform: fresh minced fish, live mealworms, a liquid "weaver ant formula" containing sucrose and human muscle-training powder, and honey solution. The 7-day study recorded food weight taken daily. The no-choice test was similarly conducted, but provided only one of the four food types to a total of 12 colonies. The choice test showed that at least one of the treatment effects was significantly greater than zero (S = 13.2; d.f. = 3; p = 0.0001; Friedman's test). Mealworms were significantly preferred over the other foods, and consumption of weaver ant formula was significantly greater than that of fish or honey ($p \geq 0.05$; Conover-Inman's test). The no-choice test showed a significant difference between at least one of the treatments (H = 8.95; d f. = 3; p = 0.03; Kruskal-Wallis test). Consumption of mealworms and fish was significantly greater than that of the liquid foods (Conover-Inman's test). Thus, mealworms were most palatable to the ants, but fish was readily accepted when no other foods were available. Mealworms and weaver ant formula were selected for a subsequent study evaluating the effect of supplemental feeding on the establishment of relocated ant colonies.

COMPARISON OF *LARICOBIUS NIGRINUS* SAMPLING METHODS AND PREVALENCE IN NATIVE AND INTRODUCED HABITATS

David L. Mausel, S.M. Salom, and L.T. Kok

Department of Entomology, Virginia Tech 216A Price Hall MC 0319,
Blacksburg, VA 24061

ABSTRACT

Beatsheet and branch clipping sampling were compared to determine which method best determined the presence or absence of *Laricobius nigrinus* Fender (Coleoptera: Derodontidae), which is being released for biological control of the hemlock woolly adelgid (HWA) (*Adelges tsugae* Annand) (Hemiptera: Adelgidae) in the eastern U.S. The total numbers of *L. nigrinus* adults collected with beatsheets or eggs and larvae by clipping branches of hemlock trees were recorded and compared with a χ^2 test or a paired t-test if abundant (n = 10 or 25). Branch clipping required the dissection of sistens HWA ovisacs to count the predator immature stages. Sites included forested release sites in Virginia, Tennessee, and North Carolina, and forested and urban forests in Washington State, within the predator's native range. *Laricobius nigrinus* presence was determined significantly more frequently or in greater absolute numbers with branch clipping than with beatsheets. At two urban forests in Washington *L. nigrinus* adults were collected from 88 and 96% of trees, eggs and larvae were collected from 100% of the trees; and eggs and larvae were collected from 44% of the ovisacs dissected. In the East, *L. nigrinus* was much less prevalent due to its recent release. In Washington, predator: prey ratios ranged from 1:2 to 1:3 in urban forests and 1:7 to 1:22 in natural forests. At release sites in the East, ratios ranged from 1:37 to 1:387. Beatsheets yielded false negatives for *L. nigrinus* presence in the East, and branch clipping is recommended. However, branch clipping required more time, and immature stages had to be identified to species by rearing, due to our inability to differentiate between *L. nigrinus* and *L. rubidus* immatures. Because each method has positive and negative aspects, we recommend using both methods at eastern release sites until *L. nigrinus* populations increase and beatsheet sampling successfully collects the predator.

COMMUNITY-LEVEL EFFECTS OF THE AMUR HONEYSUCKLE IN SOUTHWESTERN OHIO

Brian C. McCarthy

Department of Environmental and Plant Biology
Ohio University, Athens, OH 45701-2979

ABSTRACT

The Amur honeysuckle (*Lonicera maackii* (Rupr.) Maxim) (Caprifoliaceae) is one of several bush honeysuckles invading hardwood forests throughout the central and eastern United States. Other problematic species include Morrow's honeysuckle (*L. morrowii* A. Gray), Tatarian honeysuckle (*L. tatarica* L.), and Bell's honeysuckle (*Lonicera × bella*). All share a common set of morphological and ecological characteristics that make them invasive in certain habitats including high rates of seed dispersal, high seed viability, seed banking, extended morphology, disease resistance, and relatively high levels of phenotypic plasticity.

Observations in southern Ohio suggest that Amur honeysuckle is often dominant in the midstory of forests along edges and appears to be affiliated with minor disturbance. It is able to proliferate through the midstory of certain hardwood forests, displacing the native shrub flora and largely decimating the understory layer of native woody seedlings and herbs.

Several experiments were designed to evaluate the impact of Amur honeysuckle on the understory vegetation, overstory vegetation, and the impact of restoration on severely damaged forested ecosystems.

The first experiment was designed to evaluate the effects of Amur honeysuckle on vegetation, composition, structure, and diversity. We used 16 sites in southwestern Ohio: 8 from Dayton Metroparks and 8 from Cincinnati Metroparks. Most of the stands were of similar vegetation, stand history, soils, and climate. Six of the eight sites around each city contained moderate to heavy infestations of Amur honeysuckle and two served as honeysuckle-free control areas. Thus, there were 12 stands with Amur honeysuckle and 4 without.

Within each stand, we ran two parallel transects, each containing seven sample units, consisting of a modified point-center-quarter sampling unit. Thus, each stand contained 14 sample units. Each sample unit recorded the four nearest overstory trees and four nearest understory trees. Four nested quadrats were used to record the abundance of understory saplings, shrubs, woody seedlings, and herbs. Four soil samples were also obtained from each point to be used for seed-bank analysis. Finally, the four nearest Amur honeysuckles were identified and cut at ground level; dry weight biomass was determined, along with shrub age, using standard dendrochronological techniques.

From dendrochronological analysis, it was straightforward to determine when a stand had been invaded by Amur honeysuckle. In comparing the mean percent species richness for long-invaded stands vs. non-invaded stands, there was a significant decrease in virtually every structural level. The most dramatic declines occurred in the sapling (-58.2%), seed bank (-41.4%), and woody seedling (-34.9%) layers. Herb richness did not decline dramatically (-4.4%). Observations suggest that this might be due to a possible facilitation effect of Amur honeysuckle allowing other non-native species into the habitat (e.g., garlic mustard, *Alliaria petiolata*). The overstory layer, as expected, did not change in species composition (+1.4%).

Likewise, we used density as a measure of abundance and found the results quite similar to the species richness response. Regression analyses examining time since invasion (independent variable) modeled against density by layer showed a significant decline over time in the seedling, sapling, and herb layers but not in the overstory and seed bank ($\beta = 0$).

We used a multi-stratum congruence analysis to evaluate the change in species community composition. Growing literature suggests a linkage between one vegetative layer and the next. This type of analysis uses the Bray-Curtis similarity coefficient of each plot and compares the B-C similarity for the adjacent layer. This analysis revealed that there was a disintegration of the strength of linkage between layers the longer that Amur honeysuckle was found in the stand. This suggests that Amur honeysuckle will have a marked impact on the trajectory of stand succession and likely alter community dynamics for years to come.

Our second experiment was designed to determine if Amur honeysuckle was in any way impacting the overstory. Our studies to date suggested that it had no impact on the numbers of species, species composition, or density (the trees were all there before Amur honeysuckle invaded), but might there be other effects? Extensive forestry literature supports the reasoning for thinning from below. Lower strata often influence overstory productivity. Using dendrochronological techniques applied to both honeysuckle and the overstory, we were able to precisely date the time of invasion of each stand and the subsequent response of the overstory trees as measured by annual increment and basal area increment.

Using intervention analysis, we discovered that the overstory responded to invasion within 5-10 years after arrival of honeysuckle in the understory via a reduction in growth. We observed anywhere from a 5 to 30% (range; mean = 18%) decline in overstory productivity, whether adjusted by honeysuckle density or biomass. The implications of this are profound and provide a clear example of the direct negative impacts of an understory invasive species on timber economics.

Lastly, we examined different methods for Amur honeysuckle control, evaluated their efficacy and economic cost, and assessed the ability to recover a stand following invasion. This work was conducted at the Fernald Environmental Management Project outside of Cincinnati, OH. We compared two methods of honeysuckle control. One method involved traditional stem cutting and subsequent painting of the stump with herbicide (Round-up™); the other involved the use of herbicide capsule injection using the EZ-Ject Lance, which injects a capsule of herbicide (Round-up™) into the phloem and ultimately kills the tree. Both methods resulted in 99% mortality. The latter method was somewhat more costly in startup and ongoing supplies, but was able to treat a much larger area per unit time and was safer for the operator. We concluded that the EZ-Ject Lance was perhaps the best method to treat honeysuckle invasions.

Following control methods, we then in-planted a number of hardwood seedling species including black walnut, green ash, chinkapin oak, black cherry, flowering dogwood, and redbud. While survival of these species was significantly greater in treatment plots (herbicide) compared to untreated controls, we found that the ultimate survival of each species was very closely tied to the microenvironment of that site, indicating that any restoration effort involving planting of native species must very carefully match up environment and species to get a good long-term response.

In sum, Amur honeysuckle represents a significant threat to hardwood forests of the central and eastern United States. Site invasion occurs relatively quickly once the species arrives and the midstory can be subsumed within a decade. Honeysuckle will displace most native shrub, sapling, and hardwood seedlings and leads to significant declines in herb species abundance. Honeysuckle also has a marked impact on the overstory, but in a fashion quite different from lower vegetative layers. It results in the loss of overstory productivity, and this loss can be substantial. Overall, honeysuckle affects virtually every vegetative layer present. The species can be controlled, but in order for the effects to be useful, and before native vegetation declines past an irrevocable point, the species should not be left unattended in a stand for more than 10 years. Restoration in habitats that have been disturbed for longer periods of time are possible, but will require much more intensive efforts because species will need to be added manually back into the plant community.

LIVING WITH EMERALD ASH BORER: EFFECTS OF INSECT AND HOST DENSITY ON TRAPPING SUCCESS

Jessica A. Metzger[1], Ivich Fraser[2], Andrew J. Storer[1], Damon J. Crook[3], Joseph A. Francese[3], and Victor C. Mastro[3]

[1]Ecosystem Science Center, School of Forest Resources and Environmental Science
Michigan Technological University, 1400 Townsend Dr., Houghton, MI 49931

[2]USDA Animal and Plant Health Inspection Service, PPQ, Emerald Ash Borer Project
5936 Ford Court, Suite 200, Brighton, MI 48116

[3]USDA Animal and Plant Health Inspection Service, PPQ, Pest Survey,
Detection and Exclusion Laboratory, Otis Air National Guard Base, MA 02542.

ABSTRACT

Emerald ash borer (EAB) (*Agrilus planipennis Fairmaire*) (Coleoptera: Buprestidae), an invasive exotic wood-boring beetle native to regions of Asia, was first discovered on ash trees in southeastern Michigan in 2002. Since that time it has spread to and been detected in other areas of Michigan as well as in four additional states including Ohio and Indiana. Detection of EAB in areas of low population density has proven especially problematic. To date, the most effective trapping tool has involved the use of girdled trap trees. Research to develop improved detection tools for EAB has been ongoing since the beetle was first found in Michigan. Research to date has focused on chemical attractants, trap design, trap color, and ideal site selection for traps. This study aims to compare trapping technologies developed by a number of collaborating research groups at sites on a regional scale with a range of ash densities and EAB population densities. Tools tested included girdled trap trees of various ages and designs, incorporation of purple color into trap designs, and the incorporation of potentially attractive chemicals into trap designs. In the 2006 field season, the study included 62 sites distributed throughout Michigan, Indiana, and Ohio. Between 8 and 10 potential survey tools were tested at each site. Traps were established in late spring (May-June) 2006 and were monitored for adult EAB throughout the summer flight season. The health of all trap trees was evaluated in July using U.S. Forest Service protocols. In addition, trap trees were cut at each site and evaluated for the presence of EAB larvae in the fall. Preliminary analyses suggest that the effectiveness of different trap designs varies according to the density of ash at a site and the density of EAB. This study will be expanded and continued during the 2007 field season.

BEHAVIORAL RESPONSES TO ASIAN LONGHORNED BEETLE PHEROMONES

Maya Nehme[1], Kelli Hoover[1], Thomas Baker[1], Melody Keena[2], and Aijun Zhang[3]

[1]Department of Entomology, Pennsylvania State University, University Park, PA 16802

[2]U.S. Forest Service, Northern Research Station, 51 Mill Pond Rd., Hamden, CT 06514

[3]USDA Agricultural Research Service, Beltsville, MD 20705

ABSTRACT

Despite their importance, monitoring and management tools for Asian longhorned beetle (ALB) (*Anoplophora glabripennis*) have remained elusive to date. In 2002, two male-produced chemicals were isolated from ALB adults that elicited strong GC-EAD responses from both sexes of ALB. In 2005, two female-produced chemicals were also isolated from trail washes of ALB females. The volatile male-produced chemicals, one alcohol and one aldehyde, were recently tested. Four different concentrations of each chemical alone, and a 1:1 mixture of the two, were tested in a glass tube arena using a unidirectional wind. This pheromone attracted virgin females but not males, suggesting this could be a male-produced sex pheromone. The female-produced chemicals were applied in mixture in choice tests on maple twigs, where one branch was painted with the pheromone; this was repeated using maple logs divided into equal compartments. Virgin females and virgin males were tested separately. This pheromone attracted males, but was avoided by females. While further studies are planned, results suggest that tools to monitor female ALB adults in the field and to disrupt reproductive behavior are possible outcomes. Further studies will be conducted to determine the distance over which attraction occurs; field tests in China are planned for summer 2007.

DNA BASED DETECTION OF FOREST PATHOGENS

Tod Ramsfield

Ensis, Private Bag 3020, Rotorua, New Zealand

ABSTRACT

Western gall rust, caused by *Endocronartium harknessii* (syn. *Peridermium harknessii*), and pitch canker, caused by *Fusarium circinatum*, are serious pathogens of *Pinus radiata* in California and are viewed as threats to *P. radiata* in New Zealand. Forestry is the third largest export earner and a very important part of the New Zealand economy; therefore, protection of the forest estate from exotic forest pathogens is critical. The advent of the polymerase chain reaction (PCR) has allowed the development of novel DNA markers for these pathogens. PCR markers are ideal for pathogens such as rust fungi that are difficult, or impossible, to culture using traditional methods as well as fungi that are difficult or time consuming to identify using culture based morphological techniques. The DNA marker for *E. harknessii* allows identification of the pathogen within non-sporulating galls, thus speeding the identification process and thereby increasing the probability of eradication should the pathogen arrive in New Zealand. The identification of *F. circinatum* is also speeded using DNA based methods. The absence of chlamydospores is one of the diagnostic characteristics of *F. circinatum*, and cultures must be left for a minimum of 28 days to be sure chlamydospores are not produced. Using DNA markers for *F. circinatum*, it is possible to identify the pathogen in a single day. The development of novel PCR based markers is time consuming and requires access to a large DNA collection for empirical testing; however, once a robust system is developed, it is possible to screen large numbers of samples very quickly. DNA based markers should be viewed as a supplement to traditional diagnostic techniques, not as a replacement. As demonstrated by the use of the PCR technique developed at Ensis to identify *F. circinatum* on imported Douglas-fir scion material in quarantine in New Zealand (the material was subsequently destroyed), the utility of DNA based methods cannot be understated.

PROPHYLACTIC PESTICIDE APPLICATIONS AND LOW SPECIES DIVERSITY: DO THEY CREATE PEST OUTBREAKS IN THE URBAN FOREST?

Michael J. Raupp[1], Adrainna Szczepaniec[1], and Anne Buckelew Cumming[2]

[1]Department of Entomology, 4112 Plant Sciences, University of Maryland, College Park, MD 20742

[2]Urban and Community Forestry Program, U.S. Forest Service, Northern Research Station, 180 Canfield St., Morgantown, WV 26505

ABSTRACT

In light of catastrophic tree losses caused by Dutch elm disease, foresters recommended that the urban forest be diversified. The intent was to create a more sustainable urban forest that would not be decimated by a single pathogen or insect pest. However, recent introductions of deadly borers such as Asian longhorned beetle (*Anoplophora glabripennis*) and emerald ash borer (*Agrillus planipennis*) reveal that new introductions can have disastrous consequences for urban forests. We recently conducted a study to assess the threat to street trees imposed by Asian longhorned beetle and emerald ash borer in 12 cities in eastern North America if they become established and eradication programs are put into place. We collected a sample of tree inventories, identified the most common genera of trees, and enumerated the proportion of trees that might be at risk if these borers escaped quarantines and became widespread. Cities included in the study were Wilmington, DE; Chicago, IL; Lincolnshire, IL; Marion, IN; Florence, KY; Mt. Rainier, MD; Ann Arbor, MI; Kansas City, MO; New York City; Gastonia, NC; Toledo, OH; and Toronto, Canada (Raupp et al. 2006).

Thirty-two genera of trees encompassed the 10 most common trees found in the 12 cities studied (Raupp et al. 2006). The most common genus of street tree was *Acer*. Maples were found in all cities where they made up approximately 15 to 57% of the street trees (Fig. 1). The next most common genera were *Fraxinus* and *Quercus*. Both were among the 10 most common street trees in 9 of the cities inventoried. *Gleditsia*, and *Ulmus* were found in the top 10 lists for 8 of the cities, and *Malus*, *Prunus*, *Pyrus*, and *Tilia* were found in 7 lists of 10 most common

trees. Several of the most common genera encountered such as *Acer*, *Fraxinus*, *Ulmus*, and *Platanus* are known to be acceptable hosts for these exotic borers (Herms et al. 2004, Sawyer 2005).

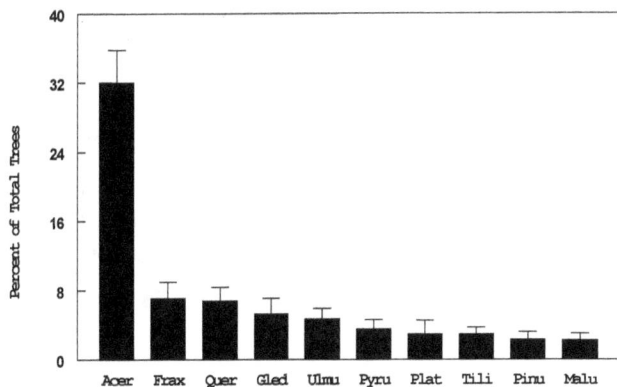

Figure 1. The 10 most common genera of street trees in 12 cities in eastern North America. Bars represent means and vertical lines represent standard errors. Acer = Acer, Frax = *Fraxinus*, Quer = *Quercus*, Ulmu = *Ulmus*, Pryu = *Pyrus*, Plat = *Platanus*, Tili = *Tilia*, Pinu = *Pinus*, Malu = *Malus*.

We suggest that losses associated with Asian longhorned beetle and emerald ash borer would be quite dramatic in terms of the proportion of trees killed, those subject to removal and replacement as part of eradication programs, and those that will require ongoing protection by one or more insecticide applications if both borers become widespread in the eastern United States. The cities included in this study face the loss or need for insecticide protection of 29 to 70% of their street trees (Raupp et al. 2006). The average percentage of trees at risk was 49.7% (4.0% s.e.). This estimate may be conservative. Recently, Morewood et al. (2003) demonstrated that red oak, *Quercus rubra*, was used for oviposition and supported larval development. They recommended that red oak be considered a potential host when surveys are conducted to detect infested trees. Host associations for Asian longhorned beetle and emerald ash borer in Asia include several genera for which no current information is available in the United States. The introduction of deadly, exotic insect pests such as Asian longhorned beetle and emerald ash borer could have devastating effects on urban forests if they escape Federal quarantines and become widespread. Urban foresters should take steps now to diversify the types of trees that are planted in cities to avoid catastrophic tree losses or massive and expensive tree protection programs.

One approach to dealing with these deadly exotic borers is to treat trees on a preventative basis with insecticides. This approach has been taken in New York City, home to one of the last great stands of American elm (*Ulmus Americana*). In 2002, Asian longhorned beetle was detected in New York City's Central Park. As part of a USDA eradication program, several thousand trees have received prophylactic treatments with the systemic pesticide imidacloprid since 2002. Since 2003, we have tracked spider mite populations on treated and untreated elms in Central Park. In each year of our study, trees treated with imidacloprid have had significantly greater densities of mites than untreated trees (Fig. 2, Raupp and Szczepaniec, unpublished).

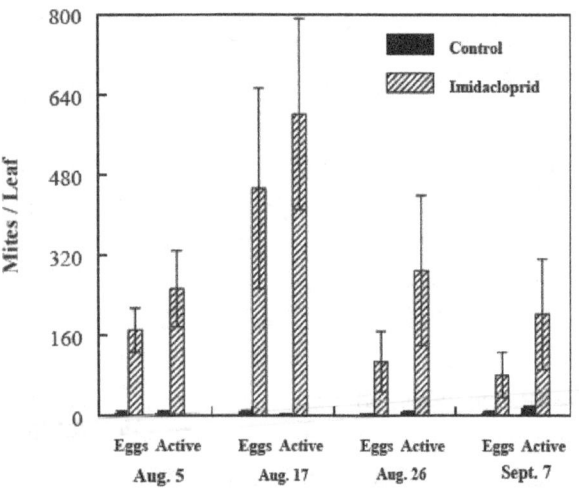

Figure 2. Abundance of *Tetranychus schoeni* on treated and untreated elms in Central Park. Bars are means and vertical lines are standard errors.

We currently have research projects underway to understand ecological processes in urban landscapes and how the disruption of these processes leads to pest outbreaks. In particular, we are elucidating the mechanisms that underlie mite outbreaks that follow the application of neonicotinoids such as imidacloprid that are used preventatively and therapeutically in eradication and management programs for exotic borers. Mite outbreaks have been reported in several systems involving landscape plants and agronomic crops. Disruption of natural enemies is one of the mechanisms proposed to explain these outbreaks (Sclar et al. 1998). In the nursery and laboratory, we will measure the effects of systemic applications of neonicotinoids on the survival and performance of important predators of spider mites: minute pirate bugs, spider mite destroyers, predatory mites, and lacewings. Also, we will test the effect of neonicotinoid exposed prey on these predators. We will survey phytophagous mites and natural enemy communities found on untreated and imidacloprid treated boxwoods, cotoneasters, and elms. A second mechanism that could underlie mite outbreaks is the stimulation of reproduction in mites caused by sublethal exposure to imidacloprid—hormoligosis (James and Price 2002). We will investigate the phenomenon of hormoligosis using three plant-spider mite associations. Finally, using plant growth measurements and phytochemical analyses, we will investigate the possibility that neonicotinoids alter the patterns of resource allocation and quality of host plants as food for mites. Our work is supported by the Tree Fund of the International Society of Arboriculture and by the National Research Initiative of the USDA Cooperative State Research, Education and Extension Service, Grant Number (2005-00915).

Literature Cited

Herms, D.A.; Stone, A.K.; Chatfield, J.A. 2004a. **Emerald ash borer: the beginning of the end of ash in North America?** In: Chatfield, J.A.; Draper, E.A.; Mathers, H.M.; Dyke, D.E.; Bennett, P.J.; Boggs, J.F., eds. Ornamental plants: annual reports and research reviews 2003. OARDC / OSU Extension Special Circular 193: 62-71.

James, D.G.; Price, T.S. 2002. **Imidacloprid boosts TSSM egg production.** Agrichemical and Environmental News. 189: 1-11.

Morewood, W.D.; Neiner, P.R.; McNeil, J.R. Sellmer, J.C.; Hoover, K. 2003. **Oviposition preference and larval performance of *Anoplophora glabripennis* (Coleoptera: Cerambycidae) in four Eastern North American hardwood tree species.** Environmental Entomology. 32: 1028-1034.

Raupp, M.J.; Buckelew Cumming, A.; Raupp, E.C. 2006. **Street tree diversity in Eastern North America and its potential for tree loss to exotic pests.** Journal of Arboriculture and Urban Forestry. 32: 297-304.

Sawyer, A.J. 2005. **Annotated categorization of ALB host trees (revised).** USDA APHIS-PPQ, Otis Pest Survey Detection and Exclusion Laboratory.

Sclar, D.C.; Gerace, D.; Cranshaw, W.S. 1998. **Observations on population increase and injury by spider mites *(Acari: Tetranychidae)* on ornamental plants treated with imidacloprid.** Journal of Economic Entomology. 91: 250-255.

INVASIVE INSECT SPECIES IN EUROPE: FIRST RESULTS OF THE DAISIE PROGRAM

Alain Roques

INRA, UR633 Zoologie Forestière, F-45166 Olivet, France

ABSTRACT

Research on insect invasions in forests became a European preoccupation only recently, and there is still no global list of exotic insects and no list of forest insect invaders available for Europe. During the past 5 years, lists of alien insects have become progressively more available in some European countries, but even more major progress is likely to result from the development since 2004-2005 of two European research projects: ALARM (Assessing Large-scale Risks with tested Methods) and DAISIE (Delivering Alien Invasive Species Inventories in Europe). The major objective of DAISIE is to deliver lists of alien organisms including insects for all European countries and the major European islands. The first results revealed the presence of more than 1,200 insect species of exotic origin in Europe and of more than 500 species of Continental Europe introduced into European islands such as UK, Malta, Corsica, and the Canary Islands. Among the exotic species, 313 are related to forests and other wooded areas such as city parks and hedgerows. Homoptera followed by Coleoptera are the dominant groups of alien insects in forests. The introduction of alien insects significantly accelerated during the second half of the 20th century; 42.4% of the species have been introduced since 1950. During the same period, Asia became the dominant source (> 20%) for exotic species establishing in Europe. Less than 2% of the forest insect invaders resulted from deliberate release (e.g., Saturnidae moths, biocontrol agents); most came as plant contaminants (77%) and a few were hitchhikers (e.g., ants, *Cameraria orhidella*). Insect species related to deciduous trees are slightly dominant compared to those specialized on conifers, but an amazingly important number of species (>50) are related to tropical trees such as eucalyptus and palm trees.

Some tendencies in arrival of alien species could also be inferred from the notifications of non-compliance regularly published by the European and Mediterranean Plant Protection Organization (EPPO). We compiled and analyzed these interception lists at the European level for 1995-2004. During this period, a total of 779 exotic forest insects were intercepted, but only 281 individuals were identified at species level for a total of 42 species. These records indicated an increasing role of bonsai in providing new forest invaders, essentially from Asia. The trade of bonsai was the source of 35.3% of the interceptions; those from wood packaging represented 37.7% (mostly from Asia). Only 24.1% of the interceptions were related to fresh wood and derivatives, mostly originating from Russia. The diversity of alien insects carried by bonsai was significantly higher than that of the entomofauna carried by wood packaging material and fresh wood. Whereas some species were relatively well represented (e.g., the cerambycids *Anoplophora* spp. and *Monohammus* spp.), a number of exotic forest insects established in Europe were never intercepted at importation such as the cerambycid *Neoclytus acuminatus*, the platypodid *Platypus mutates*, or the chestnut gall-maker (*Dryocosmus kuriphilus*). We must thus consider that a number of invasive pathways remain unknown.

Final validation of DAISIE results is planned for September 2007, followed by free Internet online access in mid- 2008.

RISK ASSESSMENT AND TREATMENT OF GARLIC MUSTARD IN MICHIGAN'S UPPER PENINSULA

Lindsey M. Shartell, Linda M. Nagel, and Andrew J. Storer

Ecosystem Science Center, School of Forest Resources and Environmental Science
Michigan Technological University, 1400 Townsend Dr., Houghton, MI 49931

ABSTRACT

Garlic mustard (*Alliaria petiolata*) is an invasive exotic biennial herb native to Europe. Where established, it can outcompete native vegetation and impact ecosystem function. Garlic mustard has been identified in the Upper Peninsula of Michigan, but is not yet widely distributed. Because of its growth characteristics, it has the potential to be a serious, widely distributed invasive weed. The objectives of this research were to test the effectiveness of control methods for garlic mustard and to determine the areas within Michigan's Upper Peninsula that are at greatest risk for invasion.

Treatments using hand-pulling, herbicide, scorching, and various combinations were applied to sites invaded by garlic mustard. The hand-pull treatment did not significantly differ in garlic mustard abundance from the control. Garlic mustard was reduced to a mean abundance of < 1 individual per 1-m^2 quadrat following herbicide, hand-pull/herbicide, scorch, and hand-pull/scorch treatments.

A spatial model is being developed to predict the areas at highest risk for invasion. The model will use garlic mustard site preferences, environmental characteristics, and human-induced factors to calculate risk levels. Accuracy of the model will be tested by comparing predictions against known garlic mustard invasions. The final maps will highlight areas at highest risk for invasion by garlic mustard, and additional maps for key areas in Upper Michigan will be produced that will aid monitoring efforts for new populations of garlic mustard.

THE EFFECTS OF ALKALOIDS ON THE FEEDING BEHAVIOR OF GYPSY MOTH LARVAE

Vonnie D.C. Shields, Kristen P. Smith, Taharah E. Shaw, Nicole S. Arnold, and Ineta M. Gordon

Biological Sciences Department, Towson University, Towson, MD 21252

ABSTRACT

Gypsy moth larvae (*Lymantria dispar* (L.)) are major pest defoliators in the United States and have been known to destroy millions of acres of trees annually. The larvae display a wide host plant preference, feeding on the foliage of hundreds of plants. They favor the leaves of deciduous hardwood trees, such as oak, sweet gum, and maple. Plants contain a variety of phytochemicals, some of which are insect feeding deterrents. These deterrents influence the food selection of many phytophagous insects including gypsy moth larvae. Deterrents, such as alkaloids, are generally not favored and are typically avoided by these larvae. In this study, we tested the effects of eight alkaloids using two-choice feeding bioassays. Each alkaloid was applied at biologically relevant concentrations to glass fiber disks and leaf disks from red oak trees (*Quercus rubra* L.), a plant species highly favored by these larvae. All eight alkaloids tested on glass fiber disks were deterrent to varying degrees. When these alkaloids were applied to leaf disks, however, only seven were still deterrent. Of these seven, five were less deterrent on leaf disks compared with glass fiber disks, indicating that their potency was dramatically reduced when they were applied to leaf disks. The reduction in deterrence may be attributed to the phagostimulatory effect of red oak leaves in suppressing the negative deterrent effect of these alkaloids, suggesting that individual alkaloids may confer context-dependent deterrent effects in plants in which they occur. We also tested the effects of these eight alkaloids at six concentrations spanning four logarithmetic steps to determine deterrent threshold effects. This study provides novel insights into the feeding behavioral responses of gypsy moth larvae to selected deterrent alkaloids. Our results may be potentially useful in designing crop protection strategies from insect pests and will help to improve our understanding of insect feeding behavior.

Supported by NIH grant 1 R15 DC007609-01 to V.S. and Bridges NIH grant 5R25GM058264-03.

PRODUCTION OF GYPCHEK IN THE WAVE® CELL CULTURE BIOREACTOR: COMPARISON TO PRODUCTION IN A STIRRED TANK BIOREACTOR

James M. Slavicek

U.S. Forest Service, Northern Research Station, 359 Main Rd., Delaware, OH 43015

ABSTRACT

A bioreactor with a completely novel design has become the bioreactor of choice by pharmaceutical companies using insect cell lines to produce proteins. This bioreactor, termed the Wave bioreactor, has several advantages compared to a stirred tank bioreactor. Methods to produce Gypchek in the Wave bioreactor were developed at 5 and 10 liter scales. Using the revertant Ld652Y cell line (described below), polyhedra production levels of approximately 4×10^{10} polyhedra per liter were found in both the 5 and 10 liter bags. This result indicates that production of virus in the Wave bioreactor will be scaleable to larger bags without a change in polyhedra production levels. A comparison of polyhedra production in the Wave vs. stirred tank bioreactors was made using the current revertant Ld652Y cell line. For these comparisons, cells from the same seed flasks were used to charge the bioreactors with cells. Consequently, the only difference in these studies was in the bioreactor used. Polyhedra production in the Wave bioreactor was found to yield higher amounts of polyhedra in all studies compared to production in the stirred tank bioreactor. Production of polyhedra in the Wave bioreactor yielded twofold more polyhedra compared to the stirred tank bioreactor. As a consequence of these results, further studies will focus on virus production in the Wave bioreactor.

During the course of our recent studies in the Wave and stirred tank bioreactors, we observed a steady significant decline in polyhedra production that stabilized at a level of about tenfold less than earlier production levels. Studies on this decline revealed that the maximum achievable cell densities in the bioreactors declined from 8×10^6 cells/ml to only 2×10^6 cells/ml, which is the reason for the drop in polyhedra production. During these studies the morphology of the Ld652Y mixed cell line changed from being primarily fibroblast-like to spherical. The new cell line became adapted to growth in suspension culture conditions and is termed suspensionLd652Y (SLd652Y). The SLd652Y cell line performs well in suspension conditions; however, it cannot achieve the necessary cell densities for economical polyhedra production. To solve this problem we are regenerating an Ld652Y cell line that is adapted for static cell growth through continuous propagation in static T-flasks. At this date, the cells have been subcultured 60 times in T-flasks, and the cell population is reverting to the original fibroblast cell line. This process is not yet complete; however, significant increases in polyhedra production have been achieved. Increases in polyhedra production of 3.5-fold and 4.0-fold have been achieved in the stirred tank and Wave bioreactors, respectively. However, for bioreactor production of virus to become operational, it is necessary to generate and use clonal cell lines that will give consistent production levels. Efforts are in progress to generate clonal *L. dispar* cell lines from available *L. dispar* cell line mixtures.

NATIVE NATURAL ENEMIES OF NATIVE WOODBORERS: POTENTIAL AS BIOLOGICAL CONTROL AGENTS FOR THE ASIAN LONGHORNED BEETLE

Michael T. Smith[1], Roger W. Fuester[1], Joseph M. Tropp[1], Ellen M. Aparicio[2], Daria Tatman[2], and Jeff A. Wildonger[2]

[1]USDA Agricultural Research Service, Beneficial Insect Introduction Research Unit
501 South Chapel St., Newark, DE 19713

[2]Department of Entomology and Wildlife Ecology, University of Delaware
Townsend Hall, Newark, DE 19711

ABSTRACT

The Asian longhorned beetle (ALB) (*Anoplophora glabripennis*) is among high-risk invasive species that have invaded the U.S. from China. ALB has attacked 25 deciduous tree species in 13 genera in North America, most notably 7 maple (*Acer*) species. Methods developed for control of *A. glabripennis* include the removal of infested trees and the use of systemic and contact insecticides. However, alternative environmentally compatible biological control methods are desired. Of particular interest are biological control agents that possess high host searching ability, particularly under low pest population levels and within species rich landscapes. Focus is also on egg and early larval instar life stages of *A. glabripennis*.

Two broad approaches are recognized for developing biological control of invasive species. The first approach is based upon natural enemies native to the countries of origin, and the second approach is based upon natural enemies native to the countries of introduction. Based upon the **first approach**, parasitoids identified from *A. glabripennis* or related *Anoplophora* species in China (Chen and He 2006) include:

1. ***Sclerodermus guani*** (Bethylidae)–Reported as a larval ectoparasitoid of *Monochamus alternatus*, *Saperda populnea*, and *Semantus sinoauster*. *S. guani* is reported to control *M. alternatus*, *S. populnea*, *S. sinoauster*, and *A. chinensis* in China, and has been evaluated against *A. glabripennis* and *A. chinensis* in China.

2. ***Dastarcus helophoroides*** (Colydiidae–Reported as a larval/pupal ectoparasitoid of 12 cerambycid species, including *A. glabripennis*, *A. chinensis*, *A. nobilis*, *Apriona germani*, *A. swainsoni*, *Botcera horsfieldi*, *Chrysobothris succudanea*, *Melanophila decastigma*, *M. alternatus*, *Trirachys orientalis*, *Xustrocera globosa*, and *Xylocopa appendiculata* (Qin and Gao 1988). However, it is not clear which of these are indigenous hosts of *D. helophoroides* and which are associated only as a result of evaluations or introductions.

3. ***Ontsira palliates*** (**Braconidae**)–Reported as a larval ectoparasitoid of *A. chinensis*, *Callidium villosulum*, *S. sinoauster*, *Metipocregyes rondoni*, *M. alternatus*, *S. populnea*, and *Xustrocera globosa*. However, it is not clear which of these are indigenous hosts of *O. palliates* and which are associated only as a result of evaluations or introductions. *O. palliates* parasitism is limited to host larvae feeding within the inner bark, implying that early larval instars may be preferred.

4. ***Zombrus*** bicolor–Reported as a solitary larval parasitoid of many cerambycid and bostrychid wood borers, including *A. chinensis*, *Batocera horsfieldi*, *Ceresium sinicum*, *Chlorophorus annularis*, *C. diadema*, *Desisa subfasciata*, Dere sp., *Nadezhdella cantori*, *Olenecampus octopusitulatus*, *S. populnea*, *Semanotus bifasciatus*, *S. sinoauster*, *Trichoferus campestris*, and *Xylotrechus pyryhoderus* (Cerambycidae), and *Bostrychopsis parallel* and *Calophagus pekinensis* (Bostrychidae).

5. ***Scleroderma sichuanensis*** (**Bethylidae**)–Reported as a larval ectoparasitoid of *Semanotus sinoauster*. Reported to control *A. chinensis*, *Clytus validus*, *M. alternatus*, *S. sinoauster*, and *S. bifasciatus* in China.

6. *Aprostocetus fukutai* (**Eulophidae**)–Reported as an egg parasitoid of *A. chinensis* and *Apriona germarii* (Liao et al. 1987, Wang and Zhao 1988).

7. *Ontsira anoplophorae* **sp. nov.** (**Braconidae**–Reported as a gregarious larval ectoparasitoid of *A. malasiaca* on citrus (Yan and Qin 1992, Zhou 1992).

8. *Ontsira sp.* (**Braconidae**)–Reported as a larval parasitoid of *A. chinensis* (Yan and Qin 1992, Zhou 1992).

However, detailed investigations of natural enemies native to China for biological control of *A. glabripennis* have focused in large part on *S. guani* Xiao Wu (Hymenoptera: Bethylidae) and *D. helophoroides* (Fairmaire) (Coleoptera: Colydiidae). Both species are ectoparasitoids of a wide range of cerambycid species that attack either deciduous or coniferous tree species. Investigations and use of these and other potential natural enemies of *A. glabripennis* have largely been limited to highly disturbed landscapes, including windrows bordering agricultural fields, rural roads in agricultural areas, monoculture plantations, and street trees in urban landscapes, where *A. glabripennis* is more commonly undergoing cyclical outbreaks. These landscapes are typically restricted to one or a few tree species, including *Populus* (poplar), *Salix* (willow), *Acer* (maple), or *Ulmus* (elm), and occasionally *Eleagnus angustifolia* (Russian-olive). The host searching efficiency of *S. guani* and *D. longulus* is unknown. Furthermore, their efficacy under *A. glabripennis* outbreak conditions within landscapes of limited tree species diversity offers limited insight into their expected efficiency in the U.S., Canada, and Europe, where *A. glabripennis* population levels are low within species rich landscapes. Therefore, before *S. guani* and *D. longulus* can be considered for release outside their country of origin, non-target studies are needed. Such non-target studies in the U.S. are awaiting receipt of import permits for these species. Additional investigations of native natural enemies of *A. glabripennis* within the countries of origin are currently focused on non-disturbed natural landscapes where it has long been found attacking native tree species under only low pest population levels.

Based upon the **second approach**, investigations of natural enemies native to the countries of introduction were initiated in North America at the USDA Agricultural Research Service Beneficial Insects Introduction Research Lab (BIIRU) in 2001 (Smith et al. 2003, 2004). Subsequently, collaborative studies between BIIRU, University of Illinois, and University of Vermont were initiated in 2003 and 2005, respectively. These studies focus in large part on species rich landscapes under low cerambycid population pressure. These studies have the following three objectives:

1. To identify and determine the relative abundance and seasonal occurrence of native cerambycids and associated natural enemy fauna infesting tree species in the Lake States, Mid-Atlantic States, and Vermont. Studies have largely focused on known *A. glabripennis* hosts (e.g., *Acer* species) and species at risk, but have also included tree species reported to harbor cerambycids.

2. To determine the effects of stress on the relative abundance and seasonal occurrence of native cerambycids and natural enemy fauna. Stress was induced at three levels: half-girdled trees (girdled 180° around the circumference), fully girdled trees (girdled 360° around the circumference), and felling.

3. To evaluate the efficacy of the native natural enemy fauna to parasitize *A. glabripennis* within infested bolts in quarantine at BIIRU.

Results reported here focus on BIIRU investigations conducted in forest stands of red maple (*Acer rubrum*), pignut hickory (*Carya glabra*), mockernut hickory (*Carya tomentosa*), and Virginia pine (*Pinus virginiana*) within the Blackbird State Forest in central Delaware. During the first year of this multiyear study, trees were stressed from July 6, 2005, to August 3, 2005. Stressed trees were inspected on a regular basis from August 2005 to December 2006 for signs of colonization (frass, oviposition scars, sap ooze, inner bark sampling). Note that our primary goal, to induce colonization by native cerambycids whose natural seasonal phenology most resembles *A. glabripennis*, aimed to obtain the associated natural enemies that might in turn parasitize *A. glabripennis* egg and early larval life stages. Therefore, at the first sign of colonization, sample bolts (52 cm) were cut from infested trees, returned to BIIRU, and caged within sono-tubes held in an outdoor insectary. Emergence from each bolt was recorded daily for all insects until November 2006. Except for potential parasitoids, all insects were preserved for identification. Potential parasitoids were bioassayed by caging an individual female wasp, normally together with a single conspecific, on *A. glabripennis* infested *A. rubrum* bolts containing egg and larval (cambium and xylem) life stages. Bioassay cages were checked daily for parental mortality and emergence of parasitoid F_1 offspring. All bioassay bolts were subsequently dissected and all *A. glabripennis* and parasitoid life stages collected and recorded.

Cerambycidae

To date, approximately 66% of the pine trees that underwent colonization were among those that had been stressed by felling, with the remaining 33% equally divided among those that had been stressed by the two girdling methods. In contrast, nearly 100% of the maple and hickory trees that underwent colonization were among those that had been stressed by felling. Although identifications are thus far tentative, results indicate that *Neoclytus mucronatus* and *Xylotrechus colonus*, *Neoclytus mucronatus* and *Neoclytus a. acuminitas*, and *Monochamus* sp. were the most abundant cerambycid species found in *C. glabra* and *C. tomentosa*, *A. rubrum*, and *P. virginiana*, respectively (Table 1). Analysis of the relative seasonal abundance of all wood borers and bark beetles has not been completed. However, *Monochamus sp.* (from pine), *Neoclytus a. acuminitas* (from maple), and *Neoclytus mucronatus* (from hickory) each showed a well-defined emergence pattern in early, mid, and late season, respectively.

Parasitoids

Results also show the relative abundance of parasitoids belonging to the Braconidae, Ichneumonidae, and Chacidoidea emerging from *C. glabra* and *C. tomentosa*, *A. rubrum*, and *P. virginiana* (Table 2). While many of the cerambycids, braconids, ichneumonids, and Chalcidoidea have been identified to genus, they are awaiting species confirmation. Analysis of the relative seasonal abundance of hymenopterous parasitoids has not been completed. Coupling detailed analysis of associated cerambycid

and bark beetle species within infested bolts and with published literature will establish parasitoid-host associations.

Bioassays

To date, most parasitoid species emerging from the 2005 field collected bolts were represented among those caged with *A. glabripennis* infested *A. rubrum* bolts in quarantine. However, among the represented hymenopterous families, the total number of individual parasitoids bioassayed was only 161, 61, and 28 individual parentals originally emerging from hickory, maple, and pine, respectively. Analysis of parental survival (duration), parasitization rate, F_1 density, and developmental rate has not yet been completed. However, at least two braconid species, including *Atanycolus* sp., and one ichneumonid species were observed displaying parasitization behavior on *A. glabripennis* infested bolts. Among these, only braconid species were found to successfully parasitize and complete development of F_1's. Furthermore, the successful braconids were largely among those whose natal host plant was *A. rubrum*. Subjectively, these results may indicate natal host plant conditioning among the braconids bioassayed. Reciprocal studies will test this hypothesis in an effort to obtain empirical (objective) data. While these results are from the first year of a multiyear study and should be considered as preliminary, these findings are significant in that they provide the first concrete evidence of a native natural enemy successfully parasitizing *A. glabripennis* and completing development outside the countries of origin.

Closing Remarks

While results to date are based upon sampling artificial stress-induced colonized trees, sampling will be expanded in 2007 to include trees undergoing naturally induced colonization. Furthermore, while results to date are based upon sampling of only the overwintering generation of woodborers and associated natural enemies, sampling will be expanded in 2007 to include the within season generations of woodborers and associated natural enemies. Finally, bioassay methods will be improved in 2007 in an effort to provide more naturally occurring conditions, e.g., environmental conditions.

Table 1. Cerambycid species colonizing (2005) and emerging from (2006) *Carya glabra* and *C. tomentosa*, *Acer rubrum*, and *Pinus virginiana*. Blackbird State Forest, Delaware. [Tentative Identification]

Tree Species	Family/Species	Total # Insects	Density (#/infested bolt)
Carya glabra & Carya tomentosa	Cerambycidae	5,982	20.3
	Neoclytus mucronatus	1,759	7.4
	Neoclytus a. acuminitas	5	1.3
	Neoclytus spp.	6	1.2
	Saperda dentatus	345	3.3
	Xylotrechus colonus	870	4.7
	Cerambycidae spp.	2,988	13.1
Acer rubrum	Cerambycidae	137	3.8
	Acanthocinus sp.	1	1.0
	Aegomorphus modestus	1	1.0
	Astylopsis macula	3	1.5
	Curius dentatus	2	1.0
	Neoclytus mucronatus	20	6.7
	Neoclytus a. acuminitas	63	3.9
	Cerambycidae spp.	46	2.2
Pinus virginiana	Cerambycidae	720	5.1
	Astylopsis collari	2	2.0
	Astylopsis macula	1	1.0
	Monochamus sp.	138	1.7
	Neoclytus mucronatus	5	2.5
	Neoclytus a. acuminitas	1	1.0
	Neoclytus spp.	1	1.0
	Xylotrechus colonus	3	1.5
	Ccrambycidae spp.	569	5.0

Table 2. Hymenoptera parasitoid species colonizing (2005) and emerging from (2006) *Carya glabra* and *C. tomentosa*, *Acer rubrum*, and *Pinus virginiana*. Blackbird State Forest, Delaware. [Tentative Identification]

Tree Species	Family/Species	Total # Insects	Density (#/infested bolt)
Carya glabra & Carya tomentosa	Braconidae	1042	4.1
	Ichneumonidae	569	2.7
	Chalcidoidea	22	1.4
Acer rubrum	Braconidac	115	3.0
	Ichneumonidae	41	1.9
	Chalcidoidea	10	3.3
Pinus virginiana	Braconidae	92	4.4
	Ichneumonidae	11	1.8
	Chalcidoidea	28	4.7

Literature Cited

Chen, Xue-xin; He, Jun-hua, eds. 2006. **Parasitoids and predators of forest pests in China.** USDA Forest Service, Forest Health Technology Enterprise Team. Beijing, China: China Forestry Publishing House. 216 p.

Liao Dingxi; Li Xueliu; Pang Xiongfei; Chen Tailu. 1987. **Hymenoptera: Chalcidoidea (1).** Economic insect fauna of China Fasc. 34. Beijing, China: Science Press. 241 p., 24 plates.

Qin Xixiang; Gao Ruitong. 1988. **Dastarcus longulus biological characteristics and its application.** Kunchongzhishi. 25(2): 109 112.

Smith, Michael T.; Yang, Zhong-qi; Hérard, Franck; Fuester, Roger; Bauer, Leah; Solter, Leellen; Keena, Melody; D'Amico, Vince. 2003. **Biological control of *Anoplophora glabripennis* (Motsch.): a synthesis of current research programs.** In: Fosbroke, S.L.C; Gottschalk, K.W., eds. Proceedings of the U.S. Department of Agriculture interagency research forum on gypsy moth and other invasive species; Annapolis, MD. Newtown Square, PA: U.S. Department of Agriculture, Forest Service, Northeastern Research Station: 87-91.

Smith, Michael T.; Fuester, Roger; Hérard, Franck; Hanks, Larry. 2004. **Prospects for inundative release of natural enemies for biological control of *Anoplophora glabripennis*.** In: Fosbroke, S.L.C.; Gottschalk, K.W., eds. Proceedings of the U.S. Department of Agriculture interagency research forum on gypsy moth and other invasive species; Annapolis, MD. Newtown Square, PA: U.S. Department of Agriculture, Forest Service, Northeastern Research Station: 55-61.

Wang Yong-jun; Zhao Zi-chen. 1988. **A preliminary study on *Aprostocetus* sp. parasitizing on *Apriona germarii* (Hope).** Kunchongzhishi. 25(6): 347-350.

Yan Junjie; QinXixiang. 1992. *Anoplophora glabripennis* (Motsch.). In: Xiao Gangrou, ed. Chinese forest insects: 455-457.

Zhou Jiaxi. 1992. *Anoplophora nobilis* **Ganglbauer.** In: Xiao Gangrou, ed. Chinese forest insects: 458-459.

BEHAVIORAL ECOLOGY OF HOST SELECTION IN THE ASIAN LONGHORNED BEETLE: IMPLICATIONS FOR SURVEYING, DETECTING, AND MONITORING ADULT BEETLES

Michael T. Smith[1], Patrick Tobin[2], Jinquan Wu[1], Weizhi He[3], Xuenong Xu[3], Gerhard Gries[4], Regine Gries[4], John H. Borden[5], Jean J. Turgeon[6], and Peter de Groot[6]

[1]USDA Agricultural Research Service, Beneficial Insect Introduction Research Unit
501 South Chapel St., Newark, DE 19713

[2]U.S. Forest Service, Northern Research Station, 180 Canfield St., Morgantown, WV 26505

[3]Chinese Academy of Agricultural Sciences-Institute of Plant Protection, Beijing, China

[4]Simon Fraser University, Burnaby, BC, Canada

[5]Pherotech Inc., Burnaby, BC, Canada

[6]Canadian Forest Service, Great Lakes Forestry Centre
1219 Queen St. East, Sault Ste. Marie, ON, Canada

ABSTRACT

The Asian longhorned beetle (ALB) (*Anoplophora glabripennis* Motschulsky) (Coleoptera: Cermabycidae) is among the high-risk invasive species that have invaded the U.S. from China. ALB has attacked approximately 25 deciduous tree species in 13 genera in North America, most notably 7 maple (*Acer*) species. To date, known infestations outside its countries of origin (year found) include New York City and Long Island, NY (1996); Chicago, IL (1998); Braunau, Austria (2001); Jersey City, NJ (2002); Gien, France (2003); Toronto, Canada (2003); Carteret, NJ (2004); Linden, NJ (2006); and Prall's Island, a part of Staten Island (2007). In addition, adult ALB were discovered in Sacramento, CA (June 2005), putting at risk many tree species in the western U.S. Infested trees continue to be found in the New York and New Jersey infestations, with 69 and 89 infested trees discovered, respectively, in the New York, and the Carteret and Linden, NJ, infestations in 2006. During 2007, a total of 80 infested trees were discovered and removed in the New York infestation as of April 22 (15 in Queens, 21 in Brooklyn, 41 on Prall's Island, and 3 on Staten Island). The total number of infested and high-risk trees removed from the North American infestations, as of April 22, 2007, includes 10,989 trees (6,184 infested) in New York City; 1,771 trees (1,551 infested) in Chicago, IL; 461 trees (113 infested) in Jersey City, NJ; 25,000 trees (600 infested) in Toronto, Canada; and 21,513 trees (616 infested) in Carteret and Linden, NJ. It should be noted that the infestation on Prall's Island is being eradicated via removal of all host trees, totaling 2,933 high-risk trees and 41 infested trees removed as of April 22.

Survey for trees infested by *A. glabripennis* depends solely on the visual inspection of individual trees by surveyors within a specified radius from trees showing signs or symptoms of attack. These visual surveys focus specifically on tree species reported to be hosts of ALB. However, the USDA Animal and Plant Health Inspection Service (APHIS) reports visual surveys to be 33-60% effective, depending upon the survey method used (i.e., ground survey, bucket truck survey, tree climber survey). Furthermore, visual surveys are very expensive, thereby limiting the number of trees inspected. To date, no methods are used specifically to detect and monitor adult *A. glabripennis* in the existing infestations in New York, New Jersey, and Chicago, such as sentinel trees or attractants. Therefore, the objectives of the research reported here were to develop (1) sentinel trees for detecting of adult ALB, (2) an attract-and-kill strategy for monitoring adult ALB, and (3) an artificial lure for detecting and monitoring adult ALB.

Sentinel Trees Studies

The objectives of the sentinel tree studies were to evaluate (1) the relative attractancy of ALB to five key tree genera used by ALB as hosts in China (*Tilia, Eleagnus, Salix, Populus,* and *Acer*); (2) the effects of wounding on the attractancy of ALB to *Acer mono* and *Acer negundo*; (3) the relative attractancy of ALB to *Acer mono, Acer platanoides,* and *Acer truncatum*; and (4) the efficacy of *Acer mono* to attract ALB from ALB-infested *Acer negundo* landscape trees and under varying ALB population levels.

Results from replicated field studies showed, to date, the following. (1) *A. glabripennis* is significantly more attracted to *A. mono* than to *Tilia paucicospapa, Eleagnus agustifolia, Salix babylonica,* and *Acer negundo*. Although the sex ratio of the background population was approximately 1:1 (F:M), female *A. glabripennis* were significantly more attracted than male *A. glabripennis* to *A. mono* at an approximate ratio of 3.5:1 (F:M). (2) *A. glabripennis* is significantly more attracted to *A. mono* than to *Acer platanoides*, the key maple species attacked in the U.S., and to *Acer truncatum*, a sister species of *A. mono* in China. (3) Wounding of *A. mono*, either produced by adult female *A. glabripennis* feeding on twigs, petioles, and leaves or by artificially simulated adult beetle feeding on twigs, significantly increased *A. glabripennis* attraction, particularly of adult female *A. glabripennis*. Although the sex ratio of the background population was approximately 1:1 (F:M), female *A. glabripennis* were significantly more attracted than male *A. glabripennis* to the wounded *A. mono* at an approximate ratio of 2:1 (F:M). Collectively, these results indicate that

A. glabripennis, particularly female beetles, are attracted to the host odors of *A. mono*. Studies also showed that *A. glabripennis* attraction to *A. mono* occurs during both peak and declining ALB population levels and that *A. mono* is capable of attracting adult beetles out of large *A. negundo* landscape trees. These results provide the basis for using *A. mono* for detection and monitoring of adult *A. glabripennis*.

Attract-and-Kill Studies

Studies were conducted to determine if potted *A. mono* trees treated with Scimitar® (an encapsulate pyrethroid) altered the attractancy of ALB to *A. mono*. Results from studies initiated in 2006 showed that ALB attraction, particularly of female ALB, was not altered by treating potted *A. mono* with Scimitar® at either 300 mg a.i. /L or 450 mg a.i. /L. Although studies will continue in 2007, these results provide the preliminary basis for using *A. mono* for monitoring adult ALB.

Artificial Lure Studies

Artificial lure studies were conducted (1) to isolate and identify the volatiles emitted by *A. mono* that are electroante-nnographically active, and (2) to identify blend(s) of *A. mono* host volatiles that are attractive to *A. glabripennis* in an olfactometer bioassay. Results from GC-EAD studies have identified a group of antennally active *A. mono* host volatiles. Additionally, results from olfactometer studies have thus far identified blend(s) of host volatiles that are significantly attractive to adult female *A. glabripennis*. Olfactometer studies are continuing and field studies will be conducted in 2007.

EFFICACY OF LAMBDA-CYHALOTHRIN FOR CONTROL OF THE ASIAN LONGHORNED BEETLE

Michael T. Smith[1], Jinquan Wu[1], Joseph M. Tropp[1], Weizhi He[2], Hongtian Su[2], Guoliang Zhang[2], Xuenong Xu[2], and Jiuning Li[3]

[1]USDA Agricultural Research Service, Beneficial Insect Introduction Research Unit
501 South Chapel St., Newark, DE 19713

[2]Chinese Academy of Agricultural Sciences-Institute of Plant Protection, Beijing, China

[3]Yanji Forest Garden, Yanji, Jilin China

ABSTRACT

The Asian longhorned beetle (ALB) (*Anoplophora glabripennis*) is among the high-risk invasive species that recently invaded the U.S. from China. The methods used to eradicate ALB within North American infestations have thus far included visual survey for ALB-infested trees, removal of ALB-infested trees, removal of all host trees within a given radius (i.e., 400 m) of known ALB-infested trees, and/or treatment, with a systemic insecticide (e.g., trunk injection, soil injection), of all host trees within a given radius (i.e., 400 m) of known ALB-infested trees. To date, over 32,000 and 23,000 high-value shade trees have been removed in the U.S. and Canada, respectively, in an effort to eradicate ALB and prevent its permanent establishment.

The objective of the research reported here was to investigate the potential development of an alternative control method based upon selective application of the pyrethroid, Lambda-Cyhalothrin, as an encapsulated insecticide under the trade names of Demand® CS or Scimitar® CS. More specifically, the objectives of the initial studies were to determine (1) the lethal dose (24 hour) and knockdown time of Lambda-Cyhalothrin, the active ingredient of Demand® and Scimitar®, applied topically to adult ALB; and (2) the residual activity of Demand® by exposing adult ALB to treated bands (Band Size: 12 x 22.5 cm²; Material: 600 X 300 Denier, 7 Mil. PVC backed polyester fabric; Source: American Home and Habitat, Inc.; Product # FPV600B; Contact www.ahh.biz). The objectives of the subsequent studies were to determine (1) the residual activity of Demand® by exposing adult ALB to treated caged *Acer mono* trees and (2) the efficacy of Demand® and Scimitar® by spraying ALB-infested *Acer negundo* street trees.

Lethal Dose and Knockdown Time of Lambda-Cyhalothrin

Results from the lethal dose studies showed that the: (a) LD_{50} = 0.13639µg/beetle (CI = 0.04717, 0.21372), and (b) LD_{90} = 0.78461µg/beetle (CI = 0.47376, 3.03056). Results from the knockdown time studies showed that the: (a) KT_{50} = 69.28298 sec (CI = 58.87043 84.27864), and (b) KT_{90} = 282.78445 sec (CI = 187.77320 624.53467).

Residual Activity of Demand® Treated Denier Bands

Demand® CS provided 100% mortality for 90 days when applied to bands at 450 mg a.i./L and 600 mg a.i./L. Additional field studies where Demand® CS is applied to bands are needed. Exposure of adult *A. glabripennis* to a lethal dose of Demand® CS is based upon several factors, including: (1) the willingness of adult beetles to walk onto and across treated bands, and (2) the number and position of bands wrapped around branches in trees at risk. We recently evaluated the willingness of adult beetles to walk onto and across different materials. Results showed that adult *A. glabripennis* most readily walked onto and across Denier, but they hesitated to walk onto burlap. We have been evaluating where adult *A. glabripennis* most commonly reside within different tree species, particularly adult female *A. glabripennis* as they lay eggs during the first year of colonization. These studies will pinpoint where bands should be placed within trees so they have the highest probability of killing adult beetles and preventing colonization.

Residual Activity of Demand® Treated Potted *Acer mono* Trees

Demand® CS, prepared in tap water at dosages of 94.0mg a.i./L, 204.24mg a.i./L, and 315.19 mg a.i./L, was applied to each of 10 potted Acer mono trees. Tap water was applied to 10 control trees. Each tree was then individually caged using hardware cloth. On the 1st, 8th, 15th, 22nd, 29th, and 36th day post treatment (DPT), two male and two female field-collected ALB were randomly introduced into each of the 40 cages. Adult beetle mortality was assessed after 24 hours. Beetles failing to exhibit leg movement when prodded with a fine brush were scored as dead. Results from the cage study indicate that Demand® CS can provide 95% and 90% 24 hour mortality for 29 days when applied to potted trees at 204.24 mg a.i./L and 315.19 mg a.i./L, respectively. However, since adult beetles were commonly found seeking refuge in cooler areas of the cage (e.g., holes or cracking in the soil surface; underneath the lip of the pots) that had not been treated with Demand® CS, these results likely underestimate the mortality that would occur on large landscape treated trees and on treated potted trees that are adequately shaded and/or where all surfaces are treated.

Efficacy of Demand® CS and Scimitar® CS Treated *Acer negundo* Urban-landscape Trees

Results showed that exposure to 300 mg a.i./L and 600 mg a.i./L Demand® CS provided overall population control of 99.0% [2765 dead/(27 live +2765 dead)] and 98.4% [2717 dead/(43 live + 2717 dead)], respectively, over the 58-day test period in 2005 (14 July to 9 September). Results also showed that exposure to 300 mg a.i./L and 600 mg a.i./L Scimitar® CS provided overall population control of 98.4% [926 dead/(15 live +926 dead)] and 98.4% [791 dead/(13 live +791 dead)], respectively, over the 67-day test period in 2006 (13 July to 17 September). This shows that Demand and Scimitar are highly effective at controlling adult ALB. However, it is important to note that the treated and check (control) plots were spatially very close to one another, and as such, the live ALB that continued to be found within the treated trees were largely due to immigration from the untreated check plots. We are confident that had the treated and check plots been farther apart and/or a treated buffer been included between the treated and check plots, it is highly probable that percent control would have been consistently maintained at ca. 100%. To obtain a direct measure of immigration, additional data analysis is currently in progress at this time: # 2005 and 2006 exit holes/tree. This will aid in determining the relative proportion of ALB within trees that resulted from emergence versus immigration. Furthermore, because our goal is to prevent oviposition by live female ALB and because ALB in Yanji, Jilin, China, have a 24- month life cycle, exit holes/tree will be evaluated in 2007 and 2008. This data will provide a measure of the efficacy of Demand® CS and Scimitar® CS to prevent attack by ALB.

Closing Remarks

Additional field studies were initiated in 2006 where Scimitar® CS is applied to potted *Acer mono* sentinel trees for detection and monitoring of adult *A. glabripennis*. Most importantly, these additional studies will determine if Demand® CS or Scimitar® CS alters the attractiveness of *A. mono* sentinel trees. For details, refer to Smith et al. on page 66 in this volume.

Literature Cited

Smith, Michael T.; Fuester, Roger W.; Tropp, Joseph M.; Aparicio, Ellen M.; Tatman, Daria; Wildonger, Jeff A. [In this proceedings]. **Native natural enemies of native woodborers: Potential as biological control agents for the Asian longhorned beetle, *Anoplophora glabripennis***. In: Fosbroke, S.L.C; Gottschalk, K.W., eds. Proceedings of the U.S. Department of Agriculture interagency research forum on gypsy moth and other invasive species; 2007 January 9-12; Annapolis, MD. Gen. Tech. Rep. NRS-P-28. Newtown Square, PA: U.S. Department of Agriculture, Forest Service, Northern Research Station.

AULACASPIS YASUMATSUI ON GUAM: THE RACE TO SAVE CYCADS

Sheri L. Smith

U.S. Forest Service, Region 5, Forest Health Protection
2550 Riverside Dr., Susanville, CA 96130

ABSTRACT

Aulacaspis cycad scale (ACS) (*Aulacaspis yasumatsui* Takagi) was first detected in Tumon, Guam in late 2003 at a hotel where *Cycas revoluta* Thunberg, a non-native ornamental cycad, and *C. micronesica* K.D. Hill, an indigenous cycad, were planted. ACS is believed to have been imported from Hawaii on ornamental cycads. ACS now infests non-native and indigenous cycads throughout Guam; severe infestations result in cycad mortality within a few months. To date, over 25% of the native cycads have died.

Cycads were the perfect low maintenance, typhoon resistant, and drought tolerant plants for Guam before the introduction of ACS. Since the scale's introduction, homeowners and landscape managers have removed many valuable plants to avoid the high level of maintenance required to prevent mortality. It appears that unabated increases of ACS populations on Guam will lead to the loss of cycads on the island. In addition to ACS, the cycad blue butterfly *Chilades pandava* (Horsfield) also non-native, was detected on Guam in July 2005. Caterpillars of this butterfly feed exclusively on young cycad foliage.

U.S. Forest Service, Forest Health Protection (FHP) funded suppression work against the scale in Guam's urban-wildland interface in 2005 and 2006. Activities were initiated too late to have an appreciable impact on the migration of scale populations throughout the island; however, some of the prominent King Sago plantings have been saved. Direct suppression efforts during 2006 concentrated on treating cycads in native forests. Both dinotefuran (soil drench) and pyriproxyfen (translaminar insect growth regulator) are being evaluated for efficacy toward ACS. Ongoing studies are focusing on evaluating additional chemicals (imidacloprid and abamectin) and methods of delivery (i.e., trunk injections), monitoring ACS populations, evaluating biological control agents (primarily predators), and conserving the genetic diversity of *C. micronesica*.

PRESERVING NATIVE CORAL TREES IN HAWAII: EFFICACY OF SYSTEMIC INSECTICIDES AGAINST THE ERYTHRINA GALL WASP

Sheri L. Smith[1] and Brian L. Strom[2]

[1]U.S. Forest Service, Region 5, Forest Health Protection
2550 Riverside Dr., Susanville, CA 96130

[2]U.S. Forest Service, Southern Research Station
2500 Shreveport Highway, Pineville, LA 71360

ABSTRACT

The erythrina gall wasp (EGW) (*Quadrastichus erythrinae* Kim) was described as a new species in 2004 from specimens collected in Singapore, Mauritius, and Reunion. Facilitated by a rapid life-cycle (~20 days) and inadvertent movement by humans, EGW is now widespread in Hong Kong, China, India, Thailand, American Samoa, Guam, Okinawa, and the Hawaiian Islands. In October 2006, EGW was detected on the continental U.S. in south Florida on *Erythrina variegata* L., a widely planted, non-native ornamental and a favorite host for EGW. *Erythrina* (coral trees) are found in tropical, subtropical, and warm temperate regions of the world and are the only known hosts for EGW.

The genus *Erythrina* includes >110 species worldwide, 24 of which are documented hosts of EGW. Most other species have not been evaluated. In North America, 18 species of *Erythrina* are native to Mexico and 2 to the U.S. mainland. Seventy species are native to the neotropics, and countless coral trees exist as high-value ornamentals in places such as San Diego and Los Angeles, CA. Many of these species are susceptible to EGW. In Hawaii EGW attacks the endemic *E. sandwicensis* O. Degener (wiliwili)

and two non-native species, *E. variegata* and *E. crista-galli, L. Erythrina,* in Hawaii are facultatively deciduous depending on availability of water, and seasonality differs among species, resulting in year-round host material for the wasp. EGW injury is so severe to wiliwili trees that their continued existence in Hawaii is in question.

Young tissues of *Erythrina*, especially leaves, shoots, and petioles, are preferred by EGW for oviposition. Severe infestations cause serial defoliation, physiological disruption, loss of seed production, and tree death. In April 2006, we began testing two chemicals (acephate and imidacloprid) and three injection systems (Arborjet, Sidewinder, and Wedgle) to evaluate their efficacy and effective duration for protecting native wiliwili trees from EGW. Trees continue to be evaluated monthly for changes in EGW infestation levels. Results of this study should aid the survival of selected wiliwili trees in Hawaii and in the development of prevention, detection, and response strategies in the face of rapid EGW range expansion in other areas of the world.

LIVING WITH EMERALD ASH BORER: THREE YEARS OF A RISK BASED SURVEY IN MICHIGAN AND WISCONSIN

Andrew J. Storer[1], Jessica A. Metzger[1], Robert L. Heyd[2], Steven A. Katovich[3], Michael D. Hyslop[1], and William R. McNee[4]

[1]Ecosystem Science Center, School of Forest Resources and Environmental Science
Michigan Technological University, 1400 Townsend Dr., Houghton, MI 49931

[2]Forestry, Fire and Mineral Management Division, Michigan Department of Natural Resources
1990 US 41 South, Marquette, MI 49855

[3]U.S. Forest Service, Northeastern Area, 1992 Folwell Ave, St. Paul, MN 55108

[4]Wisconsin Department of Natural Resources
2984 Shawano Ave., P.O. Box 10448, Green Bay, WI 54307

ABSTRACT

A risk based detection survey was initiated in Michigan in 2004 to detect outlier populations of the exotic emerald ash borer (*Agrilus planipennis*) (Coleoptera: Buprestidae). This survey was expanded to include northern Wisconsin in 2005 and all of Wisconsin in 2006. The number of sites used in this survey increased from 116 in 2004 to approximately 190 in 2006. Survey sites are concentrated in campgrounds due to the risk of the inadvertent movement of this insect in firewood. This survey uses girdled ash trap trees (*Fraxinus* spp.) to detect adults and larvae of emerald ash borer, firewood inspections to detect potential introductions of emerald ash borer, and observations of declining trees to detect existing emerald ash borer populations. A subset of trap trees established each year are left in place for reuse the following year as opposed to being cut and peeled at the end of the field season to look for larvae. In 2005, the first life stages of emerald ash borer from the Upper Peninsula of Michigan were collected as early instar larvae from a trap tree that had been established in 2004 at Brimley State Park in Chippewa County.

In 2004, emerald ash borer was found in firewood at three locations in Lower Michigan and not found on trap trees. In 2005, emerald ash borer was detected on trap trees established in 2004 and 2005 at six sites in Lower Michigan and one site (Brimley State Park) in Upper Michigan. Two additional detections in 2005 came from firewood and from inspections of declining trees. In 2006, emerald ash borer was detected on trap trees established in 2004, 2005, and 2006 at over 14 sites that had not been known to be infested.

Detection of emerald ash borer in this and other surveys is essential for management activities including those that aim to eradicate localized outlier populations and those that implement silvicultural treatments such as ash reduction to reduce damage from emerald ash borer.

THE NEW PHEROMONE DELIVERY SYSTEM
FOR GYPSY MOTH MATING DISRUPTION

Ksenia Tcheslavskaia[1], Kevin Thorpe[2], Diego Zeni[3], Carmen Bernardi[3], Agenor Mafra-Neto[3] , and Reginald Coler[3]

[1]Department of Entomology, Virginia Tech, Blacksburg, VA 24061

[2]USDA Agricultural Research Service, Beltsville, MD 20705

[3]ISCA Technologies, Inc., Riverside, CA 92507

ABSTRACT

A new gypsy moth (*Lymantria dispar* L.) (Lepidopetra: Lymantriidae) mating disruption formulation providing controlled release of Disparlure was developed by ISCA Technologies and used in both ground and aerial applications. The formulation, known as SPLAT (Specialized Pheromone & Lure Application Technology), was studied for its effect on mating success in gypsy moth populations as measured by male moth catches in pheromone-baited traps.

SPLAT was applied aerially at two dosages currently used for operational mating disruption treatments (15 and 37.5 g AI/ha). This flowable formulation, designed to be aerially applied using conventional equipment, is simple to use, rainfast, and long lasting (trap shutdown no less than 10-11 weeks); it was shown to be as effective as the Hercon Disrupt II® plastic flake formulation applied at the same dosages.

Paintballs loaded with SPLAT were used for ground application studies. All dosages (15, 50, and 75 g AI/ha) tested during the 2005 and 2006 seasons effectively disrupted mating.

ISCA Technologies plans to market SPLAT for aerial application as an alternative to the Hercon plastic flake formulation, currently used in the U.S. Forest Service Slow-the-Spread (STS) of the Gypsy Moth Program.

ALLEE EFFECTS AND GYPSY MOTH INVASIONS

**Patrick C. Tobin[1], Stefanie L. Whitmire[2], Derek M. Johnson[3],
Ottar N. Bjørnstad[4], and Andrew M. Liebhold[1]**

[1]U.S. Forest Service, Northern Research Station, 180 Canfield St., Morgantown, WV 26505

[2]Department of Agronomy and Soils, University of Puerto Rico –Mayagüez,
P.O. Box 9030, Mayagüez, PR 00681

[3]Department of Biology, University of Louisiana, P.O. Box 42451, Lafayette, LA 70504

[4]501 ASI Building, Departments of Entomology and Biology, Pennsylvania State University,
University Park, PA 16802

ABSTRACT

The ever increasing trends in global trade and international travel have increased the likelihood of arrivals of non-indigenous species, which are consequently a mounting threat to native ecosystems. Previous studies of habitat invasibility have highlighted the importance of understanding and identifying components that increase or decrease the ability of an exotic species to successfully invade a particular ecosystem. Another important aspect of invasibility is the role that Allee effects could play in the invasion process. Allee effects collectively refer to decreases in population growth rate with decreases in population abundance, and causes include the inability to locate mates, inbreeding depression, and failure to satiate predators. Allee effects can play a critical role in slowing or preventing the establishment of low density founder populations of non-indigenous species. Similarly, the spread of established invaders into new habitats can be influenced by the degree to which small founder populations ahead of the invasion front are suppressed through Allee effects (Whitmire and Tobin 2006). Understanding Allee effects can be critical in assessing extinction risks from the perspective of conservation biology, and there is growing recognition of their potentially important role during the establishment phase of biological invasions. We developed an approach to use empirical data on the gypsy moth, a non-indigenous invader in North America, to quantify the Allee threshold across geographic regions. We report that the strength of the Allee effect is subject to spatial and temporal variability, and we present what is to our knowledge the first empirical evidence that geographic regions with higher Allee thresholds are associated with slower speeds of invasion (Tobin et al. 2007).

MODELING ENVIRONMENTALLY DRIVEN LIFE CYCLES FOR HEMLOCK WOOLLY ADELGID AND THE BIOLOGICAL CONTROL AGENT *SCYMNUS SINUANODULUS*

R. Talbot Trotter and Michael E. Montgomery

U.S. Forest Service, Northern Research Station, 51 Mill Pond Rd., Hamden, CT 06514

ABSTRACT

First detected in Richmond, VA in the early 1950s, the hemlock woolly adelgid (HMA) *(Adelges tsugae)* (Hemiptera: Adelgidae) has spread to infest as many as 17 eastern states. Left untreated, infested trees may die in as little as 4 years. The HWA, like many invasive species, seems to have few natural enemies in its introduced range. This lack of natural enemies, combined with the high susceptibility of both eastern and Carolina hemlocks (*Tsuga canadensis* and *T. caroliniana*, respectively) to HWA attack, has probably facilitated its rapid expansion across the landscape. Classical biological control efforts, by which natural enemies from the invasive organism's native range are identified, reared, released, and established, can provide a long-term, low-impact, cost-effective management tool. Here, we focus on using the biology of the biological control agent *Scymnus sinuanodulus* to determine the requirements of the species so that releases are targeted to environments best suited for its establishment. This in turn should improve the odds of successful establishment. *Scymnus sinuanodulus* is a Coccinelid beetle collected in the Yunnan Province of China, where it feeds on HWA.

To identify regions of the eastern U.S. landscape where the biological control *S. sinuanodulus* is likely to establish, we built a flow model using the Stella™ modeling environment to link relationships between (1) climate (based on NOAA COOP stations), (2) the life history of the target species (HWA), and (3) the biological requirements of *S. sinuanodulus*, including temperature/ development requirements, prey availability requirements, and life history timing to simulate population dynamics over long time periods. The model was built using a modular approach in which large complex relationships are broken down into smaller nested relationships, each of which acts as a module within the model. The current state of the model suggests that some areas do provide a temperature regime that will allow *S. sinuanodulus* to complete development if its prey is available. Further work on this model should allow land managers to focus release efforts in those areas, while avoiding the costly release of beetles into areas where they are not likely to survive.

RELATIONSHIP BETWEEN THE FUNGAL PATHOGEN *ENTOMOPHAGA MAIMAIGA* AND THE GYPSY MOTH ON THE MONONGAHELA NATIONAL FOREST

Richard M. Turcotte[1] and Patrick C. Tobin[2]

[1]U.S. Forest Service, Northeastern Area, 180 Canfield St., Morgantown, WV 26505-3180

[2]U.S. Forest Service, Northern Research Station, 180 Canfield St., Morgantown, WV 26505-3180

ABSTRACT

We studied the effect of the fungal pathogen *Entomophaga maimaiga* on gypsy moth (*Lymantria dispar* L.) (Lepidoptera: Lymantriidae) populations at three sites on the Monongahela National Forest (MNF) in West Virginia from 2003 to 2006. Gypsy moth has been established on the MNF since at least 1989, and each of our study sites was located in an area defoliated by the gypsy moth in the year before this study. *Entomophaga maimaiga* is a fungal pathogen of the gypsy moth, and epizootics can lead to substantial gypsy moth mortality. We placed laboratory-reared gypsy moth larvae on soil collected from each site and measured consequent rates of infection from *E. maimaiga*. We also collected resident larvae from the sites and surveyed them for the presence of *E. maimaiga*. Infection rates of laboratory reared larvae ranged from 11 to 29 percent. In first and second instars, and third and forth instars, infection rates in field collected larvae ranged from 14 to 20% and from 25 to 100%, respectively. We were unable to detect pupae in concurrent surveys at each site. Despite the lack of pupae, and substantial mortality of gypsy moth larvae due to *E. maimaiga*, we still observed appreciable levels of defoliation (25 to 50% in the overstory canopy) in our study sites as well as in the surrounding areas. For gypsy moth management, treatments targeting gypsy moth populations may still be needed, especially to protect high-value resource areas, even when *E. maimaiga* is present and inducing significant mortality.

A SIMPLE, RAPID, AND SENSITIVE ASSAY FOR EVALUATING *BACILLUS THURINGIENSIS* STRAINS FOR THEIR INSECTICIDAL ACTIVITY TOWARD TARGET INSECTS

Algimantas P. Valaitis

U.S. Forest Service, Northern Research Station, 359 Main Rd., Delaware, OH 43015

ABSTRACT

Bacillus thuringiensis (Bt) is an aerobic, gram-positive bacterium that is used as a biopesticide for the control of lepidopteran, dipteran, and coleopteran insect pests. The insecticidal activity of Bt is mainly due to crystal (Cry) proteins produced by the bacterium during sporulation. Bt has a worldwide distribution, and a large number of different Bt strains have been isolated. These individual strains produce a variety of insecticidal Cry proteins, each of which is specific to a small group of insect species. Insect bioassays are currently used to detect and measure the insecticidal activity of Bt strains and purified insecticidal proteins derived from new Bt isolates. These bioassays are time consuming and require relatively large amounts of materials. Many factors can affect their results, including temperature, type of diet and feeding periods of the insects, and methods for evaluating the insecticidal activity. Furthermore, many insects are not very sensitive to purified Cry proteins obtained from Bt without the synergistic effect of spores, so these assays rely on assessment of growth inhibition rather than toxicity. Alternative techniques such as voltage clamping and use of cell lines or transfected cells require sophisticated equipment and expensive reagents. Receptor-based assays may not be reliable, because it has been established that binding is not sufficient for insecticidal toxicity.

During the course of the study of the mode of action of Bt in the gypsy moth, *Lymantria dispar*, it was unexpectedly discovered that the insecticidal Cry proteins induced rapid release of a membrane-bound aminopeptidase-N (APN) into the gut fluid. The amount of soluble APN can be measured quantitatively using a synthetic colorimetric substrate and a spectrophotometer. The amount of APN released was found to be dose-dependent and a reliable measure of the potency of various Bt samples.

Using this assay, we have found all insecticidal proteins tested to date induce APN release, whereas heat-denatured or inactive Bt samples do not. Furthermore, this highly sensitive assay can be used to evaluate the activity of crude Bt culture samples grown on nutrient agar plates using very small sample aliquots. The major advantages of this technique over the traditional bioassay is that it is fast (results can be obtained in hours instead of days) and highly sensitive. The sensitivity is such that it can detect the effects of sublethal doses of Bt samples. This assay overcomes a problem with the conventional assay system, when insects challenged with sublethal doses recover and produce difficulties in obtaining consistent dose-response curves.

LOCALIZATION OF THE *BACILLUS THURINGIENSIS* TOXIN RECEPTOR IN THE GYPSY MOTH BY IMMUNO ELECTRON MICROSCOPY

Algimantas P. Valaitis and Mary Ellen Kelly

U.S. Forest Service, Northern Research Station, 359 Main Rd., Delaware, OH 43015

ABSTRACT

Bacillus thuringiensis (Bt) biopesticides have proved to be highly valuable for controlling a variety of agricultural and forest insect pests. Bts are characterized by the production of insecticidal crystal (Cry) proteins, which interact with receptors on the midgut epithelial cells. After binding to their receptors, the Bt toxins insert into the membrane, form pores, and destroy the gut cells. Two Bt receptors have been identified in the gypsy moth, *Lymantria dispar*, that bind with high affinity the lepidopteran-specific Cry1A Bt toxins: a 120 kDa glycosylphosphatidyl-inositol (GPI)-anchored aminopeptidase N (APN); and a 270 kDa glyconjugate (BTR-270). Analysis of toxin binding to APN and BTR-270 by probing western blots with Cry1A toxins and by surface plasmon resonance showed that gypsy moth APN binds Cry1Ac toxin but does not interact with other Bt toxins (i.e., Cry1Aa or Cry2A toxins), which are highly toxic to the gypsy moth. In contrast, binding studies showed that BTR-270 interacts with all of these toxins, and the affinities of the toxins to BTR-270 correlate with their respective toxicities.

Immunolocalization of Bt toxin binding sites in lepidopteran insects has been previously reported. These reports have demonstrated that the Bt Cry toxins accumulate at the apical microvilli of sensitive insects. Little or no accumulation was reported in the goblet cells, cytoplasm, nucleus, or other locations. Although BTR-270 has been identified as a high-affinity receptor for Bt toxins in the gypsy moth, the localization of this Bt receptor in the insect midgut tissue has not been determined.

In this study, we used an immunogold electron microscopic procedure to study the distribution of BTR-270 in the gut tissue of third-instar and fifth-instar gypsy moth larvae. The distribution of the immunogold label for BTR-270 was essentially similar to that reported for the localization of Bt toxins in midgut tissue of lepidopteran larvae. The label was concentrated on the microvilli on the brush border membrane of midgut epithelial cells. Little or no labeling was observed in goblet cells or in the cytoplasm, confirming that BTR-270 is an intrinsic and specific component of the gypsy moth brush border membrane microvilli.

EVALUATING THE IMPACT OF INVASIVE SPECIES IN FOREST LANDSCAPES: THE SOUTHERN PINE BEETLE AND THE HEMLOCK WOOLY ADELGID

John D. Waldron[1], Robert N. Coulson[2], David M. Cairns[3], Charles W. Lafon[3],

Maria D. Tchakerian[2], Weimin Xi[2], Kier Klepzig[4], and Andrew Birt[2]

[1]Department of Environmental Studies, University of West Florida, Ft. Walton Beach, FL 32547

[2]Knowledge Engineering Laboratory, Texas A&M University, College Station, TX 77845

[3]Department of Geography, Texas A&M University, College Station, TX 77845

[4]U.S. Forest Service, Southern Research Station, Forest Insect Research, Pineville, LA 71360

ABSTRACT

The southern pine beetle (SPB) (*Dendroctonus frontalis*) (Zimn) (Coleoptera: Curculionidae) is an indigenous invasive species that infests and kills pines (*Pinus* spp.) throughout the southern U.S. The hemlock woolly adelgid (HWA) (*Adelges tsugae* (Annand) (Homoptera: Adelgidae) is a non-indigenous invasive species that infests and kills eastern hemlock (*Tsuga canadensis*) and Carolina hemlock (*T. caroliniana*) throughout their range in eastern North America. These species occur in the southern Appalachians. Herbivory by both species is of concern to forest managers, but for different reasons. In the case of the SPB, emphasis centers on forest restoration strategies, and in the case of the HWA, the concern is on predicting the impact of removing hemlock from the forest environment. Both of these issues can be investigated using a landscape simulation modeling approach. LANDIS II is a simulation modeling environment developed to predict forest landscape change over time. It is a modular, spatially explicit, landscape-scale ecological simulation model that incorporates disturbance by fire, wind, insects and pathogens, and harvesting. Because of its modular design, it has the capacity to allow for future disturbance components such as ice storms. Herein, we present a framework for using LANDIS II to evaluate the impact of herbivory by the SPB and HWA on forest landscapes in the southern Appalachians.

EVALUATION OF IMIDACLOPRID TREATMENT ON HEMLOCK WOOLLY ADELGID IN PENNSYLVANIA

S.M. Werner[1] and R.A. Cowles[2]

[1]Pennsylvania Department of Conservation and Natural Resources

[2]Connecticut Agriculture Experiment Station

ABSTRACT

The hemlock woolly adelgid (HWA) (*Adelges tsugae* Annand) has been in Pennsylvania since 1967. Currently found in 47 of 67 counties, this introduced invasive is causing significant dieback and mortality in eastern hemlock (*Tsuga canadensis* L.). The Pennsylvania Department of Conservation and Natural Resources Bureau of Forestry (PA DCNR) recently implemented a chemical suppression program to control this insect, using systemic application of imidacloprid on high- value trees on public land. As part of this program, PA DCNR treated 4,572 eastern hemlocks at 86 sites in 2005 and 7,252 trees at 30 sites in 2006. Nine imidacloprid-treated sites were selected to evaluate the efficacy of this chemical against HWA. Data were collected before and after treatment on 10 control and 10 treated trees at each site. In preliminary results, decreases of HWA were detected on treated trees relative to controls. Sites where imidacloprid was applied using soil injection had greater decreases than sites where stem injections were used, in spite of stem-injected trees having higher foliar imidacloprid concentrations. Decreases in new growth and increases in dead tips indicate a decline in hemlock health following HWA infestation, regardless of treatment activity.

INTEGRATED MODELING OF FOREST INVASIVE ALIEN SPECIES RISKS IN CANADA

Denys Yemshanov[1], Dan McKenney[1], Peter de Groot[1], Dennis Haugen[2], Vince Nealis[3], and Kevin Porter[4]

[1]Canadian Forest Service, Great Lakes Forestry Centre
1219 Queen St. East, Sault Ste. Marie, ON, Canada

[2]U.S. Forest Service, Northeastern Area, 1992 Folwell Ave, St. Paul, MN 55108

[3]Canadian Forest Service, Pacific Forestry Centre, 506 W Burnside Rd., Victoria, BC, Canada

[4]Canadian Forest Service, Atlantic Forestry Centre, 1350 Regent St., Fredericton, NB, Canada

ABSTRACT

The Canadian Forest Service has embarked on a program to help develop better risk assessment capacities for invasive alien species in Canada. This poster describes several aspects of this work including the development of specific data and models to address issues such as host availability, potential distributions of new alien species, possible spread/dispersal patterns, and cost-benefit analyses of mitigation and eradication options.

One current example of concern is *Sirex noctilio*, a wood wasp found relatively recently in both the United States and Canada. We also briefly present some preliminary results for modeling the potential spread of this species in eastern Canada. The model tracks basic population parameters such as growth rate, mortality, and viability and uses these to predict dispersal possibilities. A set of traveling wave algorithms is used to calculate the dispersal vectors and rates of spread in a landscape. The biophysical spread models are linked with GIS forest inventory databases to assess the susceptibility of landscape to infestations and track the potential spatial extent of the outbreak.

Clearly all models require appropriately humble interpretations in the face of limited knowledge on new alien species. However, it is the process of building models, rather than the models themselves, that is often most useful. Model building synthesizes knowledge, provides a quantitative framework to implement and (sometimes) test theories, and helps identify knowledge gaps and research priorities. Our overall intent is to enhance the contribution of science-based activities and modeling to address policy-relevant questions.

Baranchikov, Yuri: **Feeding and development of Siberian moth larvae on Douglas fir – favorable host for potential invader.**

Baranchikov, Yuri: **Gypsy moth reaction on pheromone concentrations in sparse and dense populations.**

Baumann, JM; Keiffer, C; Lehtoma, K; Hiremath, S: **Growth and survival of hybrid chestnut in stripland reclamation: Planting protocols using native and introduced ectomycorrhizal fungi.**

Bond, Suzanne: **Beetles invade the classroom: Introduction of a service learning curriculum to Chicago schools.**

Bordeaux, JM; Dean, JFD: **Screens for resistance to** *Amylostereum areolatum* **infection in loblolly pine (***Pinus taeda* **L).**

D'Amico, V: **An in-depth look at new viral strain for use in Gypchek.**

Doccola, JJ; Bristol, EJ; Wild, PM: **Emerging technology: trunk injection as an environmental approach to the management of destructive tree pests.**

Dodd, KJ: **Seasonal abundance of** *Sirex noctilio* **and other Siricidae captured during a large-scale delimitation survey in the northeastern United States.**

Eberhart, TL; Storer, AJ: **Living with emerald ash borer: which trees were attacked first in Michigan's Upper Peninsula?**

Eberhart, TL; Storer, AJ; Nagel, LM: **Living with emerald ash borer: Ash reduction models as silvicultural tools.**

Erbilgin, N; Wood, DL; Stein, JD; Acciavatti, R: **Evaluating lures to detect siricids infesting conifers of the Sierra Nevada and the Allegheny Mountains: Potential for trapping** *Sirex noctilio.*

Frederick, JL; Storer, AJ: **Living with emerald ash borer: Is the camping public aware of emerald ash borer and issues relating to the movement of firewood?**

Frye, MJ; Hough-Goldstein, J; Keil, CB: **Biology and host specificity of** *Gonioctena tredecimmaculata* **(Coleoptera: Chrysomelidae): a potential biological control agent for kudzu.**

Fuester, RW; Taylor, PB; Wildonger, J: **Insects contributing to ash mortality in eastern Pennsylvania.**

Grassano, S; Costa, S: **Whey-based fungal micro-factories for** *in situ* **production of entomopathogenic fungi.**

Guo, QF; Sax, Dov; Qian, H: **Poleward shifts of introduced species: joint effects of climate warming and biotic resistance?**

Hertel, Gerard D; Turner, Greg: **Invasive plants in the Gordon Natural Area.**

Hiremath, S; Lehtoma, K: **Molecular identification of ectomycorrhizal fungi associated with the American chestnut.**

Hoch, G; D'Amico, V; Solter, L; McManus, M; Zubrik, M: **Two approaches for quantifying transmission of microsporidia in semi-field conditions.**

Johnson, DM; Liebhold, AM; Tobin, PC; Bjornstad, ON: **Pulsed invasions by the gypsy moth in the US.**

Kanoti, A: **Slow-the-Spread: Maine's multi-tiered approach to managing the hemlock woolly adelgid.**

Kausrud, K; Økland, B; Skarpaas, O; Stenseth, NC; Erbilgin, N: **Spatiotemporal dynamics of invasive bark beetles – modeling dispersal strategies.**

Kohler, GR; Stiefel, VL; Wallin, KF; Ross, DW: **Predators associated with hemlock woolly adelgid (Hemiptera: Adlegidae) infested western hemlock in the Pacific Northwest.**

Lake, E; Hough-Goldstein, J: **Dispersal and impact of the mile-a-minute weevil: a 2-year study in southeastern Pennsylvania.**

Lewis, PA; Botts, MM; Molongoski, JM: **Distribution patterns of imidacloprid in saplings and large trees.**

Lichtenstein, KP; O'Hara, B; Fox, JF; Brownsmith, J; Pallette, A; Hicks, J; Dobson, JG: **Exploring ways to serve your science: providing forest threat information to a variety of audiences.**

Liebhold, A; Blackburn, L; Gottschalk, G; Luzader, G: **The Alien Forest Pest Explorer: a web-based GIS system for delivering geospatial data on invasive species.**

Lim, GT; Salom, SM; Kok, LT; Kirton, LG: **Supplemental food preference for the weaver ant,** *Oecophylla smaragdina* **(Hymenoptera: Formicidae), a potential biological control agent of the mahogany shoot borer,** *Hypsipyla robusta* **(Lepidoptera: Pyralidae).**

Mausel, DL; Salom, SM; Kok, LT: **Comparison of** *Laricobius nigrinus* **(Coleoptera: Derodontidae) sampling methods and prevalence in native and introduced habitats.**

Metzger, JA; Fraser, I; Storer, AJ; Crook, D J; Francese, JA; Mastro, VC: **Living with emerald ash borer: effects of insect and host density on trapping success.**

Montgomery, ME; Li, L; Yu, GY; Zhou, JH,; Lu, WH; Salom, S; Van Dreische, R: **Ecology of hemlock woolly adelgid and its natural enemies in China.**

Montgomery, ME; MacDonald, RC: **Establishment and efficacy of the lady beetle,** *Scymnus sinuanodulus,* **in North Carolina for biological control of** *Adelges tsugae.*

Nehme, M; Zhang, AJ; Keena, M; Baker, T; Hoover, K: **Behavioral responses to the Asian longhorned beetle pheromones.**

Onken, B; Shields, K: **HWA initiative: progress and accomplishments in 2006.**

Ott, EP; Sullivan, BT; Klepzig, KD; Schowalter, TD: **Attraction of Asian ambrosia beetle,** *Xylosandrus crassiusculus* **(Coleoptera: Curculionidae), to artificially stressed host trees.**

Robinet, C; Liebhold, A; Gray, D; Thorpe, K; Tcheslavskaia, K; Lance, D: **Lost and lonely gypsy moths: mate location failure as a mechanism causing an allee effect in the gypsy moth.**

Sanchez, V; Keena, M: **How long does it take teneral adult** *Anoplophora glabripennis* **(Coleoptera: Cerambycidae) to scleritize and then chew out of the wood?**

Shartell, LM; Nagel, LM; Storer, AJ: **Risk assessment and treatment of garlic mustard in Michigan's Upper Peninsula.**

Sills, EO; Liu, TM: **Gypsy moth slow-the-spread program: Cost-benefit assessment of the first 15 years.**

Slavicek, JM: **Production of Gypchek in the wave cell culture bioreactor: comparison to production in a stirred tank bioreactor.**

Smith, KP; Shaw, TE; Arnold, NS: **The effects of alkaloids on the feeding behavior of gypsy moth larvae.**

Smith, MT; Fuester, R; Tropp, J; Aparicio, E; Tatman, D; Wilddonger, J: **Native natural enemies of native wood-boring insects in the mid-Atlantic: potential for biological control of the Asian longhorned beetle (***Anoplophora glabripennis***).**

Smith, MT; Wu, JQ; He, WZ: **Host selection by the Asian longhorned beetle (***Anoplophora glabripennis***): sentinel / trap trees for detection.**

Smith, S: *Aulacaspis yasumatsui* **on Guam--the race to save cycads.**

Smith, S; Strom, B: **Preserving native coral trees in Hawaii: efficacy of systemic insecticides against the Erythrina gall wasp.**

Stein, J; Acciavetti, R; Erbilgin, N: **Conifer siricids of West Virginia: seasonal abundance and response to semiochemicals.**

Storer, AJ Metzger, JA; Heyd, RL; Katovich, SA; Hyslop, MD; McNee, WR: **Living with emerald ash borer: three years of a risk based survey in Michigan and Wisconsin.**

Strazanac, JS; Yang, ZQ; Wang, XY: **Biology of *Spathius agrili* Yang and emerald ash borer (*Agrilus planipennis* Fairmaire) based on field and laboratory studies in China.**

Sweeney, J; Thompson, D; Price, J; Buscarini, T; Helson, B; Meating, J: **Efficacy of imidacloprid stem injection for control of brown spruce longhorn beetle, *Tetropium fuscum* (Fabr).**

Tcheslavskaia, K; Thorpe, K; Zeni, D; Bernardi, C; Mafra Neto, A; Coler, R: **The new pheromone delivery system for gypsy moth mating disruption.**

Timms, L; Smith, S: **Does gypsy moth invasion affect the natural mortality of native caterpillars?**

Trotter III, R Talbot: **Modeling environmentally driven life cycles for hemlock woolly adelgid (Homoptera: Adelgidae) and the biological control *Scymnus sinuanodulus* (Coleoptera: Coccinellidae).**

Turcotte, RM; Tobin, PC: **Relationship between the fungal pathogen *Entomophaga maimaiga* and the gypsy moth on the Monongahela National Forest.**

Valaitis, AP: **A simple, rapid, and sensitive assay for evaluating *Bacillus thuringiensis* strains for their insecticidal activity towards target insects.**

Valaitis, AP; Kelly, ME: **Localization of the *Bacillus thuringiensis* toxin receptor in the gypsy moth by immuno electron microscopy.**

Vandenberg, JD; Castrillo, LA; Liu, H; Griggs, M; Bauer, LS: **Environmental persistence of *Beauveria bassiana* strain GHA following spray applications for control of the emerald ash borer, *Agrilus planipennis*.**

Werner, S: **Evaluation of imidacloprid treatment on hemlock woolly adelgid in PA.**

Weston, PA; Desurmont, GA: **Establishment of hemlock woolly adelgid on *Tsuga* species from western North America and Asia.**

Yemshanov, D; McKenney, D; de Groot, P; Haugen, D; Nealis, V; Porter, K: **Integrated modeling of forest invasive alien species risks in Canada.**

ATTENDEES

18th USDA INTERAGENCY RESEARCH FORUM ON GYPSY MOTH AND OTHER INVASIVE SPECIES

JANUARY 9-12, 2007
Annapolis, Maryland

Robert Acciavatti
USDA Forest Service, FHP
180 Canfield Street
Morgantown, WV 26505
racciavatti@fs.fed.us

Judy Adams
USDA Forest Service
2150 Centre Ave., Bldg. A
Fort Collins, CO 80526
jadams04@fs.fed.us

Ingrid Aguayo
Colorado State Forest Service
CSU Campus Delivery 5060
Fort Collins, CO 80523
iaguayo@colostate.edu

James Åkerson
National Park Service
3655 US Highway 211-E
Luray, VA 22835
james_akerson@nps.gov

Rich Anacker
Maryland Dept. Agriculture
50 Harry S. Truman Pkwy.
Annapolis, MD 21401
anackerRH@mda.state.md.us

Allan Auclair
USDA APHIS, PPQ
4700 River Road
Riverdale, MD 20737
allan.auclair@aphis.usda.gov

Robert Baca
USDA APHIS
4700 River Road, Unit 150
Riverdale, MD 20737
Robert.M.Baca@aphis.usda.gov

John Baggett
Fairfax County FPM Section
12055 Government Center Pkwy.
Fairfax, VA 22035
john.baggett@fairfaxcounty.gov

Philip A. Bailey
USDA APHIS
1498 Klondike Rd., Ste. 200
Conyers, GA 30094
philip.a.bailey@aphis.usda.gov

Thomas Baker
Pennsylvania State University
105 Chemical Ecology Lab.
University Park, PA 16802
tcb10@osu.edu

Yuri Baranchikov
VN Sukachev Institute of Forest
Akademgorodok
Krasnoyarsk, 660036, Russia
baranchikov_Yuri@yahoo.com

Dick Bean
Maryland Dept. Agriculture
50 Harry S. Truman Pkwy.
Annapolis, MD 21401
beanra@mda.state.md.us

Jim Bean
BASF Corporation
904 Lancelot Lane
Collierville, TN 38107
james.bean@basf.com

Robert Bedoukian
Bedoukian Research
21 Finance Dr.
Danbury, CT 06810
RHB@Bedoukian.com

Philip Bell
USDA, APHIS, PPQ
920 Main Campus Dr., Ste. 200
Raleigh, NC 27606
philip.d.bell@aphis.usda.gov

Susan Bentz
US National Arboretum
11601 Old Pond Drive
Glenn Dale, MD 20769
sbentz@ars-grin.gov

Wayne Berisford
University of Georgia
Dept. Entomology
Athens, GA 30602
berisford@bugs.ent.uga.edu

Jeff Boettner
University of Massachusetts
250 Natural Resources Road
Amherst, MA 01003
boettner@psis.umass.edu

Joyce Bolton
USDA ARS NAL
10301 Baltimore Avenue
Beltsville, MD 20705
jbolton@nal.usda.gov

Suzanne Bond
USDA APHIS
4700 River Road
Riverdale, MD 20737
suzanne.m.bond@aphis.usda.gov

Michael Bordeaux
Warnell School of Forest Resources
100 McAlpin Dr.
Winterville, GA 30683
john.bordeaux@gmail.com

Dustin Borntreger
Delaware State University
1200 DuPont Highway
Dover, DE 19901
dborntreger@desu.edu

John Bowers
Maryland Dept. Agriculture
50 Harry S. Truman Parkway
Annapolis, MD 21401
bowersJH@mda.state.md.us

Cynthia Bramon
Morris Arboretum
100 Northwestern Ave.
Philadelphia, PA 19118
bramon@pobox.upenn.edu

Kerry Britton
USDA Forest Service
1601 North Kent, RPF-7
Arlington, VA 22209
kbritton01@fs.fed.us

Ecki Brockerhoff
University of Canterbury
Private Bag 4800
Christchurch, New Zealand
eckerhard.brockerhoff@forestresearch.co.nz

Beth Buchanan
Davey Tree Expert Company
1500 N. Manuta St.
Kent, OH 44240
bbuchanan@davey.com

Rose Buckner
Maryland Dept. Agriculture
50 Harry S. Truman Pkwy.
Annapolis, MD 21401
bucknerm@mda.state.md.us

Russ Bulluck
USDA APHIS
1730 Varsity Dr., Ste. 400
Raleigh, NC 27529
russ.bulluck@aphis.usda.gov

Leon Bunce
USDA APHIS
920 Main Campus Dr., Ste. 200
Raleigh, NC 27606
leon.k.bunce@aphis.usda.gov

Layla Burgess
Clemson University
114 Long Hall
Clemson, SC 29634
laylab@clemson.edu

Barbara Burns
VT Dept. Forests, Parks & Recreation
100 Mineral St., Ste. 304
Springfield, VT 05156
barbara.burns@state.vt.us

Gabriel Cahalan
The Nature Conservancy
195 New Karner Road, Suite 201
Albany, NY 12205
gcahalan@tnc.org

Bob Cain
USDA Forest Service
740 Simms
Golden, CO 80401-4720
rjcain@fs.fed.us

Faith Campbell
The Nature Conservancy
4245 North Fairfax Drive
Arlington, VA 22203
phytodoer@aol.com

Jerry Carlson
NY State Dept. Environ. Conserv.
625 Broadway
Albany, NY 12233
jacarlso@gw.dec.state.ny.us

Randolph Ciurlino
Delaware Dept. Agriculture
2320 S. DuPont Highway
Dover, DE 19901
randolph.Ciurlino@state.de.us

Tom Coleman
University of Georgia
413 Biological Sciences
Athens, GA 30602
colemant@uga.edu

Reg Coler
ISCA Technologies, Inc.
2060 Chicago Ave., #C-2
Riverside, CA 92507
ISCA@ISCATech.com

Karen Coluzzi
Maine Dept. Agriculture
28 State House Station
Augusta, ME 04333
karen.l.coluzzi@maine.gov

Scott Costa
University of Vermont
206 Hills Bldg.
Burlington, VT 05492
scosta@uvm.edu

Robert Coulson
Texas A&M University
Dept. Entomology
HEEP Center, Room 408
College Station, TX 77843
r-coulson@tamu.edu

John Crowe
USDA APHIS
15 Iron Road
Hermon, ME 04401
john.f.crowe@aphis.usda.gov

Robert Daley
University of Pittsburgh, CS
5401 Sennott Square
Pittsburgh, PA 15260
daley@cs.pitt.edu

Vince D'Amico, III
USDA Forest Service
c/o University of Delaware
Newark, DE 19717
vdamico@elbowfarm.com

Peter deGroot
Canadian Forest Service
1219 Queen Street
Sault Ste. Marie, Ontario
pdegroot@nrcan.gc.ca

Thomas Denholm
NJ Dept. Agriculture
638 Sixth St.
Atco, NJ 08004
tom.denholm@ag.state.nj.us

Don Diamond
JJ Mauget Co.
5435 Peck Road
Arcadia, CA 91006
mary@mauget.com

Andrea Diss-Torrance
Wisconsin Dept. Nat. Resources
P.O. Box 7921
Madison, WI 53707
andrea.disstorrance@wi.gov

Mary Ellen Dix
USDA Forest Service
1601 North Kent St.
Arlington, VA 22209
mdix@fs.fed.us

Joseph Doccola
Arborjet, Inc.
99 Blueberry Hill Rd.
Woburn, MA 01801
joedoccola@arborjet.com

Kevin Dodds
USDA Forest Service
271 Mast Road
Durham, NH 03824
kdodds@fs.fed.us

Nathan Dodds
JJ Mauget Co.
5435 Peck Road
Arcadia, CA 91006
mary@mauget.com

Alan K. Dowdy
USDA APHIS
4700 River Road, Unit 26, 5C-03G
Riverdale, MD 20737
alan.k.dowdy@aphis.usda.gov

Marla Downing
USDA Forest Service
2150 Centre Ave., Bldg. A, Ste. 331
Fort Collins, CO 80526
mdowning@fs.fed.us

Jeff Drake
USDA APHIS
New Mexico State University
Las Cruces, NM 88003
jefdrake@nmsu.edu

Wes Drosselmeyer
USDA APHIS
P.O. Box 66
Inwood, WV 25428
wesley.l.drosselmeyer@aphis.usda.gov

Don Duerr
USDA Forest Service
1720 Peachtree Rd. NW
Atlanta, GA 30309
dduerr@fs.fed.us

Don Eggen
Pennsylvania Bureau of Forestry
208 Airport Drive
Middletown, PA 17057
deggeg@state.pa.us

Joseph Elkinton
University of Massachusetts
Fernald Hall
Amherst, MA 01003
elkinton@ent.umass.edu

Roeland Elliston
USDA APHIS, PPQ
2150 Centre Avenue
Ft. Collins, CO 80526
roeland.j.elliston@aphis.usda.gov

Nadir Erbilgin
University of California-Berkeley
140 Mulford Hall
Berkeley, CA 94704
erbilgin@nature.berkeley.edu

Wilson Faircloth
USDA ARS
P.O. Box 509
Dawson, GA 39842
wfaircloth@nprl.usda.gov

Charles Ferree
The Nature Conservancy
11 Ave. DeLafayette
Boston, MA 02111
cferree@tnc.org

Gavin Ferris
University of Delaware
92 Blake Road
Elkton, MD 21921
gkferris@udel.edu

Frank Finch
Fairfax County FPM Section
12055 Government Center Pkwy.
Fairfax, VA 22035
frank.finch@fairfaxcounty.gov

Heather Finch
Fairfax County Urban Forest Mgmt.
12055 Government Center Pkwy.
Fairfax, VA 22035
heather.finch@fairfaxcounty.gov

Joel Floyd
USDA APHIS, PPQ
4700 River Road, Unit 137
Riverdale, MD 20737
joel.p.floyd@aphis.usda.gov

James Fox
University of North Carolina
Rhoades 201, CPO #2345
Asheville, NC 28804
jfox@unca.edu

Susan Frankel
USDA Forest Service
800 Buchanan St.
Albany, CA 94710
sfrankel@fs.fed.us

Ivich Fraser
USDA, APHIS, PPQ
5936 Ford Ct., Ste. 200
Brighton, MI 48116
ivich.fraser@aphis.usda.gov

Matthew Frye
University of Delaware
531 S. College Avenue
Newark, DE 19716
mfrye@udel.edu

Robert Fusco
Valent Bioscience
HC 63
Mifflintown, PA 17059
robert.fusco@valent.com

Roger W. Fuester
USDA-ARS, BIIRL
501 S. Chapel Street
Newark, DE 19713
roger.fuester@ars.usda.gov

Jeff Garnas
Dartmouth College
Gilman Hall 210
Hanover, NH 03755
jeff.garnas@dartmouth.edu

Lynn Garrett
USDA APHIS
1730 Varsity Drive, Ste. 400
Raleigh, NC 27606
lynn.j.garrett@aphis.usda.gov

Michael Geryk
Massachusetts Dept. Cons. & Rec.
P.O. Box 484
Amherst, MA 01004
michael. geryk@state.ma.us

Lindsey Gibson
Delaware State University
1200 DuPont Highway
Dover, DE 19901
lgibson@desu.edu

Bruce Gill
Canadian Food Inspection Agency
960 Carling Ave., K.W. Neatby Bldg.
Ottawa, Ontario K1A 0C6
gillbd@inspection.gc.ca

Nancy Gillette
USDA Forest Service
P.O. Box 245
Berkeley, CA 94701
ngillette@fs.fed.us

Ken Gooch
Massachusetts Dept. Conserv./Rec.
740 South St., PO Box 1433
Pittsfield, MA 01202
ken.gooch@state.ma.us

James Gooder
USDA Forest Service
359 Main Road
Delaware, OH 43015
jgooder@fs.fed.us

Kurt Gottschalk
USDA Forest Service
180 Canfield Street
Morgantown, WV 26505
kgottschalk@fs.fed.us

Svetlana Gouli
University of Vermont
661 Spear Street
Burlington, VT 05405
sgouli@uvm.edu

Vladimir Gouli
University of Vermont
661 Spear Street
Burlington, VT 05405
vgouli@uvm.edu

David Gray
Canadian Forest Service
P.O. Box 4000
Fredericton, NB, Canada E3B 5P7

Matthew Greenstone
USDA ARS
BARC-West, Bldg. 011A
Beltsville, MD 20705
greenstm@ba.ars.usda.gov

Jean-Claude Grégoire
Université Libre de Bruxelles
Lubies, CP 160/12
1050 Brussels, Belgium
jcgregoi@ulb.ac.be

Mike Griggs
USDA ARS
Tower Road
Ithaca, NY 14853

Dawn Gunderson-Rindal
USDA ARS
BARC-West, Bldg. 011A
Beltsville, MD 20705
gundersd@ba.ars.usda.gov

Quinfeng Guo
USDA Forest Service
200 WT Weaver Blvd.
Asheville, NC 28804

Tony Guitierrez
US Army CHPPM
Aberdeen Proving Ground, MD
tony.gutierrez@amedd.army.mil

Kevin Hackett
USDA ARS, National Program Staff
5601 Sunnyside Avenue
Beltsville, MD 20705
kjh@ars.usda.gov

Ann Hajek
Department of Entomology
Cornell University
Ithaca, NY 14853
aeh4@cornell.edu

Richard Hallett
USDA Forest Service
271 Mast Road
Durham, NH 03824
rah@unh.edu

Betsie Handley
Maryland Dept. Agriculture
5303 Spectrum Dr. Ste. F
Frederick, MD 21703
mdacent@erols.com

Bill Hargrove
USDA Forest Service
102 Westover Drive
Oak Ridge, TN 37830
hnw@fire.essd.ornl.gov

Heather Harmon
Delaware Dept. Agriculture
2320 S. DuPont Highway
Dover, DE 19901
heather.harmon@state.de.us

PJ Hart
Hardwood Federation
1111 19th Street NW
Washington, DC 20036
p.hart@hardwoodfederation.com

Nathan Havill
Yale University
Dept. Ecology & Evolutionary Biol.
New Haven, CT 06520
nathan.havill@yale.edu

Deborah Hayes
Maryland Department of Agriculture
50 Harry S. Truman Pkwy.
Annapolis, MD 21401
debhayes@dmv.com

Jim Heath
Hercon Environmental
P.O. Box 435
Emigsville, PA 17318
jheath@herconenviron.com

Izzy Heller
Bedoukian Research
21 Finance Drive
Danbury, CT 06810
izzy@Bedoukian.com

Kara Hempy-Mayer
Colorado Department of Agriculture
700 Kipling Street, Ste. 4000
Lakewood, CO 80215
kara.hempy-mayer@ag.state.co.us

Jonathan Hickman
SUNY at Stony Brook
650 Life Sciences Bldg.
Stony Brook, NY 11794
jhickman@gmail.com

Jeff Hicks
University of North Carolina
Rhoades 201, CPO #2345
Asheville, NC 28804
jmhicks@gmail.com

Shelley Hicks
Maryland Department of Agriculture
50 Harry S. Truman Pkwy.
Annapolis, MD 21401

Yasutomo Higashiura
Hokkaido Forest Research Inst.
Bibai, Hokkaido
079-0198 Japan
yasu@fri.bibai.hokkaido.jp

Gernot Hoch
BOKU – University of Natural Resources
Hasenauerstrasse 38
A-1190 Vienna, Austria
hoch@ento.boku.ac.at

E. Richard Hoebeke
Dept. Entomology, Comstock Hall
Cornell University
Ithaca, NY 14853
erh2@cornell.edu

Carol Holko
Maryland Department of Agriculture
50 Harry S. Truman Pkwy.
Annapolis, MD 21401
holkoca@mda.state.md.us

Kelli Hoover
Dept. Entomology, 543 ASI Bldg.
Pennsylvania State University
University Park, PA 16802
kxh25@psu.edu

Judy Hough-Goldstein
University of Delaware
531 S. College Avenue
Newark, DE 19716
jhough@udel.edu

Cynthia Huebner
USDA Forest Service
180 Canfield Street
Morgantown, WV 26505
chuebner@fs.fed.us

Leland Humble
Canadian Forest Service, NRC
506 W. Burnside Road
Victoria, British Columbia V8Z 1M5
lhumble@pfc.forestry.ca

Merideth Humphries
Dept. Entomology, 543 ASI Bldg.
Pennsylvania State University
University Park, PA 16802

Roy Hunkins
University of Massachusetts
250 Natural Resources Rd.
Amherst, MA 01003

Lisa Jackson
USDA APHIS
1730 Varsity Drive, Ste. 400
Raleigh, NC 27606
lisa.d.jackson@aphis.usda.gov

Derek Johnson
University of Louisiana
Lafayette, LA 70504
derekjohnson@louisiana.edu

Kyrre Kausrud
Norwegian Forest & Landscape Inst.
Box 115
1431 Ås, Norway
kyrreka@blo.uio.no

Melody Keena
USDA Forest Service
51 Mill Pond Rd.
Hamden, CT 06514
mkeena@fs.fed.us

Craig Kellogg
USDA APHIS, PPQ
5936 Ford Ct., Ste. 200
Brighton, MI 48116
craig.kellogg@aphis.usda.gov

Bridget Kelly
e2M
2751 Prosperity Ave.
Fairfax, VA 22031
Bkelly@e2M.net

Kathleen Kidd
NC Dept. Agriculture
1060 Mail Service Center
Raleigh, NC 27699
kathleen.kidd@ncmail.net

Troy Kimoto
Canadian Food Inspection Agency
4321 Still Creek Dr., Fl. 4, Rm. 400
Burnaby, British Columbia V5C 6S7
kimotot@inspection.gc.ca

Philipp Kirsch
APTIV
PO Box 417
Marylhurst, OR 97036
semiochem@aol.com

Karen Kish
West Virginia Dept. Agriculture
1900 Kanawha Blvd.
Charleston, WV 25305
kkish@ag.state.wv.us

Carolyn Klass
Cornell University
4140 Comstock Hall
Ithaca, NY 14853
ck20@cornell.edu

Brian Kopper
USDA APHIS
920 Main Campus Dr.
Raleigh, NC 27606
brian.j.kopper@aphis.usda.gov

Lane Kreitlow
NCDA – Plant Industry Division
1060 Mail Service Center
Raleigh, NC 27699
lane.kreitlow@ncmail.net

Jimmy Kroon
Delaware Dept. Agriculture
2320 S. DuPont Highway
Dover, DE 19901
jimmy.kroons@state.de.us

Craig Kuhn
Maryland Dept. Agriculture
P.O. Box 502
Forest Hill, MD 21050
nefpm@hotmail.com

Nancy Kummen
Canadian Food Inspection Agency
1905 Kent Rd.
Kelowna, British Columbia V14 7S6
Kummenn@2inspection.gc.ca

Kerrie Kyde
Maryland Dept. Natural Resources
580 Taylor Avenue, E-1
Annapolis, MD 21401
kkyde@dnr@state.md.us

James LaBonte
Oregon Dept. Agriculture
635 Capitol St., NE
Salem, OR 97301
jlabonte@oda.state.or.us

Ellen Lake
University of Delaware
531 South College Ave.
Newark, DE 19716
elake@udel.edu

Ashley Lamb
Virginia Tech
216 Price Hall, Entomology
Blacksburg, VA 24061
aslamb@vt.edu

David Lance
USDA, APHIS, PPQ
Bldg. 1398
Otis ANGB, MA 02542
david.r.lance@aphis.usda.gov

Deborah Landau
The Nature Conservancy
5410 Grosvenor Lane, Ste. 100
Bethesda, MD 20850
dlandau@tnc.org

William Laubscher
Pennsylvania DNR - FPM
208 Airport Drive
Middletown, PA 17057
wlaubscher@state.pa.us

Steven Lavallee
USDA APHIS
222 Holiday Dr., Ste. 1
White River Junction, VT 05001
stephen.g.lavallee@aphis.usda.gov

Danny Lee
USDA Forest Service
P.O. Box 268D
Asheville, NC 28802
dclee@fs.fed.us

Donna Leonard
USDA Forest Service, FHP
200 WT Weaver Blvd.
Asheville, NC 28802
dleonard@fs.fed.us

Christopher Lettau
Wisconsin Dept. Agriculture
2811 Agriculture Dr.
Madison, WI 53718
christopher.lettau@datcp.state.wi.us

Phil Lewis
USDA APHIS, PPQ
Bldg. 1398
Otis ANGB, MA 02542
philip.a.lewis@aphis.usda.gov

Karin Lichtenstein
University of North Carolina
Rhoades 201, CPO #2345
Asheville, NC 28804
klichten@unca.edu

Andrew Liebhold
USDA Forest Service
180 Canfield Street
Morgantown, WV 26505
aliebhold@fs.fed.us

Tzu-Ming Liu
North Carolina State University
707 Mannington Dr.
Morrisville, NC 27560
Tliu3@ncsu.edu

Gary Lovett
Institute of Ecosystem Studies
Box AB, 65 Sharon Tnpke.
Millbrook, NY 12545
lovettg@ecostudies.org

Tom Lupp
Maryland Dept. Agriculture
5303 Spectrum Dr., Ste. F
Frederick, MD 21703
mdacent@erols.com

Suzanne Lyon
University of Massachusetts
Ag Engineering Bldg.
Amherst, MA 01003
slyon@psis.umass.edu

Barry Lyons
Canadian Forest Service
1219 Queen Street East
Sault Ste. Marie, Ontario P6A 2E5
blyons@nrcan.gc.ca

Martin MacKenzie
USDA Forest Service
180 Canfield Street
Morgantown, WV 26505
mmackenzie@fs.fed.us

Priscilla MacLean
Hercon Environmental
P.O. Box 435
Emigsville, PA 17318
pmaclean@herconenviron.com

Rory MacLellan
Canadian Food Inspection Service
RR #2 Black Horse Corner
Kensington, PEI C0B 1M0
maclellanrf@inspection.gc.ca

John Maerz
University of Georgia
Warnell School
Athens, GA 30602
jmaerz@warnell.uga.edu

Stephen Malan
Maryland Dept. Agriculture
50 Harry S. Truman Pkwy.
Annapolis, MD 21401
malansc@mda.state.md.us

Mary Kay Malinoski
Maryland Coop. Ext. Svc.
12005 Homewood Road
Ellicott City, MD 21042
mkmal@umd.edu

Tim Marasco
Pennsylvania Bureau of Forestry
208 Airport Drive
Middletown, PA 17057
tmarasco@state.pa.us

Jose Marcelino
University of Vermont
661 Spear Street
Burlington, VT 05401
jmarceli@uvm.edu

Ken Marchant
Canadian Food Inspection Agency
174 Stone Road West
Guelph, Ontario N1G 4S9
marchantk@inspection.gc.ca

Debra Martin
Virginia Dept. Agriculture
102 Governor Street, Room LL55
Richmond, VA 23219
Debra.Martin@vdacs@virginia.gov

Victor C. Mastro
USDA, APHIS, PPQ
Bldg. 1398
Otis ANGB, MA 02542
vic.mastro@aphis.usda.gov

Brian McCarthy
Ohio University
Porter Hall, 416b
Athens, OH 45701
mccarthy@oak.cats.ohiou.edu

Beth McClelland
Virginia Dept. Agriculture
102 Governor Rd., Room LL55
Richmond, VA 23219
beth.mcclelland@vadcs.virginia.gov

Max W. McFadden
The Heron Group, LLC
P.O. Box 741
Georgetown, DE 19947
mcfadden@dca.net

Michael McManus
USDA Forest Service
51 Mill Pond Road
Hamden, CT 06514
mlmcmanus@fs.fed.us

Joel McMillin
USDA Forest Service
2500 S. Pine Knoll Dr.
Flagstaff, AZ 86001
jmcmillan@fs.fed.us

Pat Michalak
USDA APHIS
13611 Crawford Ave.
Blue Ridge Summit, PA 17214
patricia.s.michalak@aphis.usda.gov

Bruce Miller
Pennsylvania State University
P.O. Box 406
North East, PA 16428
bjmiller@psu.edu

Dan Miller
USDA Forest Service
320 Green Street
Athens, GA 30602
dmiller03@fs.fed.us

Michael Montgomery
USDA Forest Service
51 Mill Pond Road
Hamden, CT 06514
memontgomery@fs.fed.us

Steve Munson
USDA Forest Service
4746 S. 1900 E.
Ogden, UT 84403
smunson@fs fed.us

George Nelson
USDA APHIS
326 Mercer Corporate Park
Robbinsville, NJ 08691
george.j.nelson@aphis.usda.gov

Ellen Nibali
University of Maryland
12005 Homewood Rd.
Ellicott City, MD 21042
enibali@umd.edu

Larry Nichols
Virginia Dept. Agriculture
P.O. Box 1163
Richmond, VA 23218
larry.nichols@vdacs.virginia.gov

Rebecca Nisley
USDA Forest Service
51 Mill Pond Rd.
Hamden, CT 06514
rnisley@fs.fed.us

Larry Norton
Bayer
4233 Harriet Lane
Bethlehem, PA 18017
larry.norton@bayercropscience.com

Bjørn Økland
Norwegian Forest & Landscape Inst.
Box 115
1431 Ås, Norway
bjorn.okland@skogoglandskap.no

William Oldland
USDA Forest Service
180 Canfield Street
Morgantown, WV 26505
woldland@fs.fed.us

Brad Onken
USDA Forest Service
180 Canfield Street
Morgantown, WV 26505
bonken@fs.fed.us

Andrei Orlinski
EPPO
1, Rue le Nôtre
75016 Paris, France
orlinski@eppo.fr

Richard Orr
National Invasive Species Cncl.
1201 I Street NW
Washington, DC 20005
richard.orr@ios.doi.gov

Eric Ott
LSU Ag Center
342 Jennifer Jean Dr.
Baton Rouge, LA 70808
eott@agcenter.lsu.edu

Imre Otvos
Canadian Forest Service
506 W. Burnside Rd.
Victoria, British Columbia V8Z 1M5
iotvos@pfc.forestry.ca

Nicholas Padowski
SUNY, Environ. Science & For.
1 Forestry Drive
Syracuse, NY 13210
napadows@syr.edu

April Pallette
University of North Carolina
Rhoades 210, CPO #2345
Asheville, NC 28804
peacewthinl@aol.com

Patrick Parkman
University of Tennessee
2431 Joe Johnson Dr.
Knoxville, TN 37996
jparkman@utk.edu

Bradley Parks
University of Colorado
P.O. Box 1288
Boulder, CO 80466
bradley.parks@colorado.edu

Dylan Parry
SUNY, Environ. Science & For.
1 Forestry Drive
Syracuse, NY 13210
dparry@esf.edu

Randall Peiffer
Delaware State University
1200 DuPont Highway
Dover, DE 19901
rpeiffer@desu.edu

Scott Pfister
VT Dept. Forests, Parks, & Recr.
103 South Main St., Bldg. 10 S.
Waterbury, VT 05671
Scott.pfister@state.vt.us

Michael Philip
Michigan Dept. Agriculture
PO Box 30017
Lansing, MI 48909
philipm@michigan.gov

Therese Poland
USDA Forest Service
1407 S. Harrison Rd.
East Lansing, MI 48823
tpoland@fs.fed.us

John Podgwaite
USDA Forest Service
51 Mill Pond Road
Hamden, CT 06514
jpodgwaite@fs.fed.us

Jean-Luc Poupart
Canadian Food Inspection Agency
59 Camelot Dr.
Ottawa, Ontario K1A 0Y9
poupartj@inspection.gc.ca

Evan Preisser
University of Rhode Island
100 Flagg Rd.
Kingston, RI 02881
preisser@uri.edu

Robert Rabaglia
USDA Forest Service
1601 N. Kent St., RPC-7
Arlington, VA 22209
brabaglia@fs.fed.us

Tod Ramsfield
ENSIS
Private Bag 3020
Rotorua, New Zealand
tod.ramsfield@ensisjv.com

Carol Randall
USDA Forest Service
3815 Schreiber Way
Coeur d'Alene, ID 83815
crandall@fs.fed.us

Michael Raupp
University of Maryland
Department of Entomology
College Park, MD 20742
mraupp@umd.edu

Richard Reardon
USDA Forest Service, FHTET
180 Canfield Street
Morgantown, WV 26505
rreardon@fs.fed.us

Steve Rehner
USDA ARS
Bldg. 011A, BARC-West
Beltsville, MD 20705
rehners@bc.ars.usda.gov

Laurie Reid
South Carolina Forestry Commission
5500 Broad River Road
Columbia, SC 29210
lreid@forestry.state.sc.us

James Rhea
USDA Forest Service
200 W.T. Weaver Blvd.
Asheville, NS 28804
rrhea@fs.fed.us

Kim Rice
Maryland Dept. Agriculture
50 Harry S. Truman Pkwy.
Annapolis, MD 21401
riceka@mda.state.md.us

Artemis Roehrig
University of Massachusetts
250 Natural Resources Rd.
Amherst, MA 01003
a_roehri@skidmore.edu

Alain Roques
INRA
Zoologie Forestière
BP 20619
Ardon 45166 Olivet, France
Alain.roques@orleans.inra.fr

Darrell Ross
Oregon State University
College of Forest Science
Corvallis, OR 97330
Darrell.ross@oregonstate.edu

Mark Ross
Ministry of Forestry
PO Box 2526
Wellington, New Zealand
Mark.ross@maf.govt.nz

Kathleen Ryan
University of Toronto
33 Willocks St.
Toronto, Ontario M5S 3B3
kathleen.ryan@utoronto.ca

Scott Salom
Virginia Tech
216 Price Hall
Blacksburg, VA 24061
salom@vt.edu

Laura Samson
Alphawood Foundation
2451 N. Lincoln Ave., #205
Chicago, IL 60614
lsamson@alphawoodfoundation.org

Frank Sapio
USDA Forest Service
2150 Centre Ave., Bld. A, Ste. 331
Ft. Collins, CO 80526
fsapio@fs.fed.us

Taylor Scarr
Ministry of Natural Resources
70 Foster Drive, Ste. 400
Sault Ste. Marie, Ontario P6A 6V5
taylor.scar@mnr.gov.on.ca

Nathan Schiff
USDA Forest Service
PO Box 227
Stoneville, MS 38776
nschiff@fs.fed.us

Noel Schneeberger
USDA Forest Service
11 Campus Blvd., Ste. 200
Newtown Square, PA 19073
nschneeberger@fs.fed.us

Jean Scott
Mauget Company
5435 Peck Rd.
Arcadia, CA 91006
mary@mauget.com

Ronald Sequeira
USDA APHIS
1017 Main Rd.
Raleigh, NC
Ron.a.sequeira@aphis.usda.gov

Troy Shaw
Fairfax County FPM Section
12055 Government Center Pkwy.
Fairfax, VA 22035
troy.shaw@fairfaxcounty.gov

Loretta Shields
Canadian Food Inspection Agency
14154 Niagara River Parkway
Niagara, Ontario L0S 1J0
shieldsl@inspection.gc.ca

Vonnie Shields
Towson University
8000 York Rd.
Towson, MD 21252
vshields@towson.edu

Michael Simon
USDA APHIS
4700 River Road, Unit 60
Riverdale, MD 20737
michael.simon@aphis.usda.gov

James Slavicek
USDA Forest Service
359 Main Road
Delaware, OH 43015
jslavicek@fs.fed.us

Bryan Smalley
Timber Products Services
P.O. Box 919
Conyers, GA 30012
bsmalley@tpinspection.com

Gibbs Smith
USDA APHIS
930 Main Campus Dr.
Raleigh, NC 27606
gibbs.l.smith@aphis.usda.gov

M. Alex Smith
Biodiversity Institute of Ontario
University of Guelph
Guelph, Ontario
salex@uoguelph.ca

Sheri Smith
USDA Forest Service
2550 Riverside Dr.
Susanville, CA 96130
ssmith@fs.fed.us

John Snitzer
Hood College
P.O.Box 38
Dickerson, MD 20842
navajuela@comcast.net

Lee Solter
Illinois Natural History Survey
1101 W. Peabody Dr., Box 18
Urbana, IL 61801
lsolter@uiuc.edu

Dennis Souto
USDA Forest Service
271 Mast Road
Durham, NH 03824
dsouto@fs.fed.us

Sven-Erik Spichiger
PA Bureau of Forestry, DCNR
208 Airport Drive, 2nd Floor
Middletown, PA 17057
sspichiger@state.pa.us

John Stein
USDA Forest Service
180 Canfield Street
Morgantown, WV 26505
jstein@fs.fed.us

Jeffrey Stibick
USDA APHIS
4700 River Road
Riverdale, MD 20737
jeffrey.stibick@aphis.usda.gov

James Stimmel
Bureau of Plant Industries
2301 N. Cameron Street
Harrisburg, PA 17110
jstimmel@state.pa.us

Andrew Storer
Michigan Tech University
1400 Townsend Dr.
Houghton, MI 49971
storer@mtu.edu

John Strazanac
West Virginia University
Ag. Sci. Bldg., Evansdale Dr.
Morgantown, WV 26506
jstrazan@wvu.edu

Brian Strom
USDA Forest Service
2500 Shreveport Highway
Pineville, LA 71360

Brian Sullivan
USDA Forest Service
2500 Shreveport Highway
Pineville, LA 71360
briansullivan@fs.fed.us

Jil Swearingen
National Park Service
4598 MacArthur Blvd. NW
Washington, DC 20007
jil_swearingen@nps.gov

Jon Sweeney
Canadian Forest Service
29 Sprucewood Dr.
New Maryland, NB, Canada E3C 1C6
jsweeney@nrcan.gc.ca

Bob Tatman
Maryland Department of Agriculture
50 Harry S. Truman Pkwy.
Annapolis, MD 21401
nefpm@erols.com

Mark Taylor
Maryland Department of Agriculture
50 Harry S. Truman Pkwy.
Annapolis, MD 21401
taylormc@mda.state.md.us

Philip Taylor
USDA ARS
501 S. Chapel St.
Newark, DE 19713
philip.taylor@ars.usda.gov

Ksenia Tcheslavskaia
Dept. Entomology
Virginia Tech
Blacksburg, VA 24061
ktchesla@vt.edu

Steve Teale
State University of New York
Environmental Science & Forestry
Syracuse, NY 13210
sateale@esf.edu

Justin Thaxton
USDA APHIS
Rt. 1, Box 142
Ripley, WV 25271
justin.b.thaxton@aphis.usda.gov

Harold Thistle
USDA Forest Service
180 Canfield St.
Morgantown, WV 26505
hthistle@fs.fed.us

Kevin Thorpe
USDA, ARS, BARC-West
10300 Baltimore Ave.
Beltsville, MD 20705
Thorpe@ba.ars.usda.gov

Robert Tichenor
Maryland Dept. Agriculture
50 Harry S. Truman Pkwy.
Annapolis, MD 21401
tichenrh@mda.state.md.us

Steve Tilley
Maryland Department of Agriculture
50 Harry S. Truman Pkwy.
Annapolis, MD 21401
fpmes@ccisp.net

Laura Timms
University of Toronto
33 Willocks Street
Toronto, Ontario M5S 3B3
laura.timms@utoronto.ca

Patrick Tobin
USDA Forest Service
180 Canfield Street
Morgantown, WV 26505
ptobin@fs.fed.us

Matthew Travis
Maryland Dept. Agriculture
50 Harry S. Truman Pkwy.
Annapolis, MD 21401
travisma@mda.state.md.us

R.Talbot Trotter
USDA Forest Service
51 Mill Pond Road
Hamden, CT 06514
rttrotter@fs.fed.us

Robert Trumbule
Maryland Dept. Agriculture
6701 Lafayette Ave.
Riverdale, MD 20737
rtrumbule@erols.com

Richard Turcotte
USDA Forest Service
180 Canfield Street
Morgantown, WV 26505
rturcotte@fs.fed.us

Jake Urian
Delaware State University
1200 N. DuPont Highway
Dover, DE 19901
jurian@desu.edu

John Vandenberg
USDA ARS
Tower Road
Ithaca, NY 14853
jdv3@cornell.edu

Roy VanDriesche
University of Massachusetts
Fernald Hall, Entomology
Amherst, MA 01003
vandries@nre.umass.edu

David Wagner
University of Connecticut
461 TLS Building
Storrs, CT 06269
David.wagner@uconn.edu

Karen Walker
Prince William County
4092 Merchant Plaza, Ste. A
Woodbridge, VA 22192
kwalker@pwcgov.org

Liz Warner
Maryland Dept. Agriculture
5303 Spectrum Dr., Ste. F
Frederick, MD 21703
mdacent@erols.com

Shahla Werner
PA Bureau of Forestry, DCNR
208 Airport Drive, 2nd Floor
Middletown, PA 17057-5027
shawerner@state.pa.us

Paul Weston
Cornell University
150 Insectary
Ithaca, NY 14853
paw23@cornell.edu

Geoffrey White
USDA ARS, Bldg. 007, Rm. 301
10300 Baltimore Avenue
Beltsville, MD 20705
whiteg@ba.ars.usda.gov

Jacob Wickham
SUNY, CESF, 241 Illick Hall
1 Forestry Drive
Syracuse, NY 13210
jdwickha@syr.edu

Brian Widener
New Jersey Forest Service
26 Central Avenue
New Brunswick, NJ 08901
bwidener@njfscf@gmail.com

Jeff Wildonger
USDA ARS
501 S. Chapel Street
Newark, DE 19713
donger@udel.edu

Benjamin Wolfe
Harvard University
16 Divinity Avenue
Cambridge, MA 02138
bwolfe@oeb.harvard.edu

Hirofumi Yamaguchi
Hokkaido Forest Research Inst.
Bibai, Hokkaido
079-0198 Japan

Larry Yarger
USDA Forest Service
1601 N. Kent Street, RPC
Arlington, VA 22209
larger@fs.fed.us

Denys Yemshanov
Canadian Forest Service
1219 Queen Street East
Sault Ste. Marie, Ontario P6A 2E5
dyemshan@nrcan.gc.ca

Heping Zhu
USDA ARS
1680 Madison Avenue
Wooster, OH 44691
Zhu.16@osu.edu

Gottschalk, Kurt W., ed. 2008. **Proceedings, 18th U.S. Department of Agriculture interagency research forum on gypsy moth and other invasive species 2007**; 2007 January 9-12; Annapolis, MD. Gen. Tech. Rep. NRS-P-28. Newtown Square, PA: U.S. Department of Agriculture, Forest Service, Northern Research Station. 99 p.

Contains 60 abstracts and papers of oral and poster presentations on gypsy moth and other invasive species biology, molecular biology, ecology, impacts, and management presented at the annual U. S. Department of Agriculture Interagency Research Forum on Gypsy Moth and Other Invasive Species.